Aimee Semple McPherson

Aimee Semple McPherson

Read the True Story!

Canadian-born evangelist
One of America's most popular personalities!

Douglas H. Rudd

Guardian BOOKS

Belleville, Ontario, Canada

Aimee Semple McPherson.
1890 – 1944.

Aimee Semple McPherson

Copyright © 2006, Douglas H. Rudd

Cover: Aimee Semple McPherson at her finest. Angelus Temple, Los Angeles, California, a church still vibrant today.

The photos appearing on the front and back covers and in chapters 3, 9, 11, 13, 20, 21, 24 and 25 supplied by The Heritage Department of the International Church of the Foursquare Gospel are used with permission of the Heritage Department.

All scripture quotations, unless otherwise indicated, are taken from The New King James Version. Copyright © 1982 by Thomas Nelson, Inc., Publisher. Used by permission. All rights reserved. • Scripture quotations marked KJV are taken from *The Holy Bible, King James Version.* Copyright © 1977, 1984, Thomas Nelson Inc., Publishers. • Scripture quotations marked NASB are taken from the *New American Standard Bible*, copyright © The Lockman Foundation 1960, 1962, 1963, 1968, 1971, 1972, 1973. All rights reserved.

Library and Archives Canada Cataloguing in Publication

Rudd, Douglas H. (Douglas Haig), 1919-
  Aimee Semple McPherson : read the true story! / Douglas H. Rudd.

ISBN 1-55452-070-3. --ISBN 1-55452-071-1 (LSI ed.)

  1. McPherson, Aimee Semple, 1890-1944. 2. Evangelists--United States--Biography. 3. International Church of the Foursquare Gospel--Clergy--Biography. 4. Evangelists--Canada--Biography. I. Title.

BX7990.I68M3 2006a   289.9   C2006-903354-4

For more information, please contact:

Antioch Books
Box 62102 Burlington Mall P/O
Burlington, ON L7R 4K2
ruddbooks@sympatico.ca

Guardian Books is an imprint of *Essence Publishing,* a Christian Book Publisher dedicated to furthering the work of Christ through the written word. For more information, contact:

20 Hanna Court, Belleville, Ontario, Canada K8P 5J2.
Phone: 1-800-238-6376 • Fax: (613) 962-3055.
E-mail: publishing@essencegroup.com
Internet: www.essencegroup.com

Table of Contents

Acknowledgments

I wish to acknowledge and thank all of those people who have shown an interest and encouraged me in this writing project.

Deep appreciation and thanks to my son, Robert Rudd, an editor by profession, who freely edited and proofread the material, giving valuable advice in the overall undertaking. "Thanks, Bob."

Thank you to Marilyn Stroud, Assistant Archivist at the Pentecostal Assemblies of Canada (PAOC) headquarters, who, in addition to proofreading, located key articles containing vital information. Thank you, as well, to proofreader Ralph Hodgson of Burlington, Ontario.

Thanks to Dennis Molyneaux of Crossroads Family of Ministries for his computer expertise.

Thanks to The International Church of the Foursquare Gospel and Janet Simonsen, Heritage Department Manager, for graciously providing helpful information and pictures and permission to publish same.

Thanks to Dr. Jack Hayford, Foursquare President, for his personal note of encouragement.

Thanks for reassurance from Dr. Edith Blumhofer, historian, lecturer and author of *Aimee Semple McPherson— Everybody's Sister*, published by William B. Eerdmans Publishing Company, Grand Rapids, Michigan. She has, in my estimation, written the finest and most complete account of Mrs. McPherson's life. This current volume fills a niche for a smaller book, with a different layout and some new pictures. I have drawn heavily from Dr. Blumhofer's book.

Thanks to Essence Publishing of Belleville, Ontario, Publishing Manager Rikki-Anne McNaught and Project Editor Cindy Thompson for their cooperation and expertise in this whole project.

Finally, thank you to my dear wife, Margaret, for her daily encouragement.

Douglas Rudd
2006

Preface

The purpose of this book is to present a true, up-to-date account of Aimee Semple McPherson's life and ministry. She left no doubt that her life's primary focus was evangelism when she said:

Soul winning is the most important thing in the world. All I have is on the altar of the Lord, and while I have life and strength, I will put my whole being into carrying out the Great Commission.[1]

A. C. Valdez Sr., a contemporary of hers, succinctly described her gifts and achievements as follows:

God never left a mold behind to make others like Aimee Semple McPherson. How the Holy Spirit used her! She was many things in the Lord, including perpetual motion and seeming omnipresence. She never appeared to stop evangelizing. Thousands of souls were introduced to Christ by her.

I recall Aimee's charisma, personal charm, physical attractiveness, liquid fluency with words, and her ability to present the gospel in simple terms.

Then she founded Angelus Temple—a splendid home for God, and His people, seating 5,300 and distinctive for its lofty dome, the life of Jesus told in stained-glass windows, and dramatic red carpeting.

Aimee preached four things—salvation in Jesus, Holy Spirit baptism, healing, and the second coming of

Christ. These four points were the basis of the worldwide Foursquare Gospel Churches which she founded.[2]

These quotes aptly portray the person and work of Aimee Semple McPherson.

Introduction

In early childhood I heard Aimee Semple McPherson's name mentioned in our home. At that time I did not know who she was or what she did. Aimee was born near Ingersoll, Ontario, Canada, about fifty miles from my own birthplace.

In researching her life, I became aware of the need for an updated, concise volume. Unfortunately, many accounts of her life have faulty conclusions based on old newspaper clippings from inaccurate and biased sources. In the 1920s, six Los Angeles newspapers vied for the latest "scoop."

This book seeks to present an accurate account throughout, rather than a diatribe of innuendoes that have sullied the reputation of a good person.

A Celebrity

In the early 1920s, Aimee Semple McPherson, a Canadian farm girl turned evangelist, burst upon the American horizon. She rivaled Mary Pickford, Douglas Fairbanks and Charlie Chaplin in both popularity and ability. Her name was on the lips of thousands across North America.

Just how well known she became was evident to me during World War II, while I was serving in the army. War was being waged on several fronts around the world. One morning in the fall of 1944, I was sitting at my desk just outside the company commander's office. Suddenly, we heard the colonel coming down the hall. I immediately called the orderly room staff to attention as he passed through our office and into his own. No sooner did he sit down at his desk than the major, his second-in-command, stepped into the colonel's office from a side door. The first words the colonel uttered were, "Aimee Semple McPherson is dead." He might have bid the major good morning, commented on the progress of the war or weather, but no; it was about Mrs. McPherson's death far away. These two men, both professionals, but not overly religious, considered word of her death world news even twenty years after the peak of her popularity.

Subject Matter

This book gives a panoramic view of Aimee's childhood, conversion, call to ministry, marriage, rise to fame, kidnapping, escape, vindication and the legacy she left. Her sermons were positive and upbeat, portraying God's love and mercy. Multiplied thousands of people were drawn to God through her ministry.

Glad tidings of great joy to all people! (See Luke 2:10.)

1. Early Life

Aimee's maiden name was Aimee Kennedy. She was born on October 9, 1890, in her parents' home, about five miles south of the town of Ingersoll, set in the richly productive farmland of southwestern Ontario, Canada.

When Mrs. Gibbs, the midwife, brought the little newborn downstairs and presented her to James Kennedy, her father, no one dreamed of the vast potential wrapped up in that tiny bundle. Heritage and environment both contribute to the making of a person. The dominant personality of Aimee's mother, Minnie, and James' practical ingenuity were both blended in Aimee, but her latent talent and power to achieve far exceeded that of any family member. There was a special charisma about her.

The Kennedy Family

Aimee's father, James, was a descendant of early settlers from the United States, some of whom were United Empire Loyalists. Ingersoll was linked to Port Burwell on Lake Erie by a primitive thirty-one-mile road of planks and gravel that gave access to outside markets for their produce. In 1851, the village of Salford sprang up at a bend in the road near the Kennedy farm. Soon there was a Methodist church, a Baptist church, a school and a sawmill.

Like others in that area, the Kennedys engaged in a variety of mixed farming. There were also dairy farmers who helped in the development of the famous Ingersoll Cheese factory.

Aimee was born in 1890 when life in southwestern Ontario revolved around agriculture. The area shown is where she would begin her effective service as a Christian evangelist.

The Kennedy lineage boasted generations of Methodists. James and his first wife, Elizabeth, were both active members of the Salford Methodist church. It is believed that James sang in the choir and sometimes played the organ. A successful farmer, he also had a knack for building anything from houses to bridges. They had three children, Mary Elizabeth, Wallace and Charles. Winter evenings would often be spent gathered about the pump organ singing Scottish-Irish folk songs and old hymns of the church.

In March of 1886, Elizabeth took seriously ill. By that time their daughter had married and Charles had died of tuberculosis. Wallace was later killed in an accident. It was a household of sorrow. Elizabeth needed extra care, so James hired Mildred (Minnie) Ona Pearce, a Salvation Army teenager from Lindsay, Ontario, who was traveling in the area with the Army. Minnie nursed Elizabeth and cared for household chores. Apparently she proved to be capable and dependable, because, after Elizabeth's death, James asked Minnie to marry him, despite the difference in their ages.

Minnie's Heritage

We are greatly indebted to Dr. Edith L. Blumhofer for her biography of Aimee, already referred to. In it she delves into the Ontario background of both James and Minnie. She tells of life and activity in the Lindsay corps of the Salvation Army and gives an insight into the Army's dedication and impact on the social and religious life of a community. Minnie had been deeply involved in the activities of the Lindsay corps and brought the same dedication to Ingersoll. This environment helped prepare Aimee for her future. The Salvation Army's rigid lifestyle, plus the zeal of the Pentecostals and power of the Holy Spirit, helped to mold Aimee for her life's work.

Early Training

Minnie's prayer for a daughter was fulfilled in Aimee, whom Minnie loved, sheltered and mentored. James doted on her too, and shared with her his love for both nature and music.

Minnie instilled within the child a love and respect for spiritual things with Bible stories and scriptural memorization, and Aimee was quick to learn.

Her greatest role model in ministry and style came from Evangeline Booth, the daughter of William Booth, the Salvation Army's founder. Evangeline was gifted, dramatic, irrepressible and energetic. She led with dedication and flare. Her illustrated sermons must have inspired young Aimee. Evangeline was the Salvation Army's Commissioner for

Canada from 1896 to 1904. One of her most dramatic portrayals, entitled "Miss Booth In Rags," depicting rescue work in the slums of London, England, was staged in Toronto's famous Massey Hall.

A New Home

In 1897, James rented out the house that was Aimee's birthplace and built a new spacious frame house a few hundred yards east. Minnie's uncle in Lindsay sent a carload of lumber as a gift. Apparently there was prosperity on both sides of the family. Minnie named the new home Kosy Kot. Knowing Minnie's penchant for hospitality, the new home was probably the site of many social events for the neighborhood. All of this would prepare Aimee to move with ease in society.

School Days

Aimee was enrolled at No. 3 Dereham Public School, in September 1896. She soon proved herself adept at public speaking and won a gold medal in a contest sponsored by the Women's Christian Temperance Union. It also became evident that Aimee was a born leader. In September 1905, she entered high school at the Ingersoll Collegiate Institute where the course of study set a high standard in academics. But here she was introduced to Darwin's theory of evolution. It came as a rude shock when she realized that the acceptance of Darwin's theory meant the rejection of the biblical account of God's creation.

As Aimee was in the throes of decision, she read a letter in The Family Herald and Weekly Star submitted by Bishop Hamilton of Ottawa, Ontario. The bishop strongly and ably opposed evolution being taught in the schools and his reasoning appealed to Aimee.

One winter evening as Aimee pondered the matter, she gazed out of her window into a clear moonlit sky and marveled at the vast expanse of starry heavens. She came to the conclusion that only God could have created the universe. She also wrote a letter to the editor. Her letter was deemed a remarkable work for a teenager. Throughout her life, she maintained a strong view of God's hand in creation.

Worldliness

Aimee had lived a life sheltered from worldly events and amusements, but as she grew older she began to move in adult social circles, getting a taste of the so-called freedom that others seemed to enjoy. A strong pull developed between the strict standards of her mother, Minnie, and the lure of the world. Something had to give, and soon.

2. Transformed

Aimee became more and more involved with acting, elocution, charades and other activities. Her schedule for the Christmas season of 1907 was filled with several events, one of which was a play at the Ingersoll Town Hall in which she had a leading role. But something happened that would forever alter her whole outlook.

The Sign in a Window

It was just an ordinary sign in a storefront window, but it was one that would begin to change Aimee's life and affect thousands of others after her. Two words stood out at the top, "Pentecostal Mission." That name would be unfamiliar to most people of the time. A few might connect it with the coming of the Holy Spirit on the Day of Pentecost, but modern Pentecostals were just coming on the scene at that time.

Aimee's father had come to town with horse and cutter to bring her home from the collegiate. When Aimee saw the sign, she suggested to her father that when he brought her to town for practice that night she would like to go and see a Pentecostal meeting for herself. She had heard strange things about the meetings and thought it would be fun to watch.

Dropping in on a Revival

They took a back seat and, sure enough, it was just as she had heard. The people said "Amen" and "Hallelujah." Dressed in her finery, Aimee felt a cut above most of them, but that attitude was also about to change. Aimee sat and smiled as she observed it all—that is, until it came time for the sermon.

Then she saw a tall young man stand with a Bible in his hand and begin to read from the latter part of Acts 2. She was captivated as he spoke with a soft Irish accent, taking his text from the 38th and 39th verses,

Repent, and be baptized every one of you in the name of Jesus Christ for the remission of sins, and ye shall receive the gift of the Holy Ghost. For the promise is unto you, and to your children, and to all that are afar off, even as many as the LORD our God shall call (KJV).

The preacher exhorted them to repent of their sins and receive the baptism in the Holy Spirit. Then he paused, closed his eyes and spoke briefly in another tongue as the Spirit gave him utterance. To Aimee, it was the voice of God. *"Let's go, Daddy, quickly,"* she whispered to her father, and they slipped out.

Convicted

What Aimee had heard disturbed her. For three days she was in turmoil. As an only child, she had been petted and pampered, but now she felt the searchlight of God's Holy Spirit shining into the deep recesses of her soul. Would she submit and yield her will to God or not? It felt like a life and death matter. She must have often heard similar appeals to give her life to Christ in the Salvation Army, but had not repented and yielded her will and her life to the Lord.

Three days later, as she was driving home from school on a bleak afternoon, she came to the end of her willful way. Throwing up her hands and dropping the horse's reins she cried aloud, *"Lord God, be merciful to me, a sinner."* (See Luke 18:13.)

Converted

That was it! The burden was lifted and into her heart flowed joy and love. She began to sing consecration hymns she knew so well, such as Frances Havergal's "Take my life and let it be consecrated, Lord, to Thee" and so on. "Take my feet... my voice...my lips." Totally surrendered to the will of God, a peace surpassing all understanding flooded her soul. It was the dawning of a new day. In place of a novel under her pillow was the Bible. And she found herself frequenting the Pentecostal Mission as often as possible.

The Baptism in the Holy Spirit

Aimee soon learned about the "Promise of the Father," the Holy Spirit baptism that Jesus had promised His disciples. She developed such a deep hunger to receive all that God had for her that she even skipped some periods from school to wait before God at the mission. Reports of her activities reached her parents. Would she be forbidden to attend the mission? Then, unexpectedly, the way opened for her to spend even more time there.

One morning the country roads were blocked by snow, so Aimee took the train to school in Ingersoll. Even the locomotive found it difficult to buck the deep snow drifts. The blizzard increased and the tracks were blocked. She would not be able to get home until the storm abated and the tracks were cleared. One of the ladies from the mission opened her home to Aimee and there she waited before the Lord in prayer and consecration. For two wintry days she was shut in with the opportunity to seek the Lord.

On Saturday morning she came downstairs and went into the parlor to pray. She knelt down at a large Morris chair in the corner, determined to seek God. Taking Luke's Gospel, chapter 11, as her guide, she noted that Jesus used three words in teaching how to pray—*ask*, *seek* and *knock*. She was especially encouraged by verse 13, where He said that if an earthly father gives good gifts to his children, "*how much more will your heavenly Father give the Holy Spirit to those who ask Him!*"

It was so clear. Instead of begging God for His Holy Spirit, she began to praise Him. The more she praised Him, the closer He came. Her whole soul was swept up into the presence of the Lord when suddenly, out of her innermost being, rivers of praise began to flow and she started to speak in another tongue. The Lord had baptized her in His Spirit. Like many others, she found a new love for God, for His Word and for other people. The next day was Sunday, and she went to the mission and partook of communion in the morning service.

An Ultimatum

When her daughter hadn't returned home, Minnie decided to go to town and fetch Aimee herself. During the long ride home Minnie vented her anger, but Aimee seemed to show no remorse and instead she hummed and sang a well-known Army song,

Joys are flowing like a river,
Since the Comforter has come...

When neither Minnie nor James could "talk sense" into Aimee, they banished her to her room. Next morning, Minnie issued an ultimatum: Aimee would be kept home from school for good if she mingled with the Pentecostals again. Instead of being intimidated, Aimee countered with her own proposal: If Minnie could show from the Bible that the Pentecostals were wrong, then Aimee would never associate with them again. Minnie took up the challenge and sat down at the table with her Bible, paper and pencil, to settle the matter.

When Aimee returned home at night Minnie was still at the table, but she was more subdued and admitted that the Bible seemed to be on the Pentecostals' side. It wasn't long until mother and daughter were hugging one another and singing joyfully, "*Give me that old-time religion.*"

3. Calling and Marriage

For Aimee, those were days of heaven upon earth. Early Pentecostals loved to congregate by the hour to study the Bible and worship the Lord. Often they gathered about a piano or organ and lifted their voices in songs of consecration and adoration. Alone at home, Aimee sat at the piano playing and singing over and over again words such as,

I'll go where You want me to go, dear Lord,
O'er mountain or plain or sea;
I'll say what You want me to say, dear Lord,
I'll be what You want me to be.

Aimee's Call to Ministry

One day as she was praying alone in her bedroom, Aimee sensed that God was drawing her attention to words similar to those in Jeremiah 1:4-9:

Before I formed thee in the belly I knew thee; and before thou camest forth out of the womb I sanctified thee, and I ordained thee a prophet unto the nations. Then said I, Ah, Lord GOD! behold, I cannot speak: for I am a child. But the LORD said unto me, Say not, I am a child: for thou shalt go to all that I shall send thee, and whatsoever I command thee thou shalt speak. Be not afraid of their faces: for I am with thee to deliver thee, saith the LORD. Then the LORD put forth his hand, and touched my mouth. And the LORD said unto me, Behold, I have put my words in thy mouth (KJV).

At first it seemed too astounding and impossible to be true that the Lord would ever call such a simple, unworthy country girl as she to go out and preach the gospel. It seemed wonderful, almost unbelievable.

How Could it Be?

Aimee was sure the call had come from God, but where and how was she to begin? Then the answer came from an unexpected source. One evening she was sitting with some sick children in the same home where she had received the baptism in the Spirit. The door opened, and in walked Robert Semple. He had heard that the children were ill and had come over to sit up with them. "*But that's what I am doing,*" Aimee asserted, so they both sat with them. Robert prayed for the children and soon they were sleeping peacefully.

Robert went on to tell Aimee of his call to carry the gospel to China. Then it was Aimee's turn to tell him that she too had received a call from the Lord, but where she did not know. She was not hinting to be connected with his ministry. Nothing was further from her mind, until she found her hand held firmly in his and heard him saying, "*That is just what I came to talk to you about. Aimee, dear, will you become my wife and go with me to China?*" They both knelt in prayer to ask the Heavenly Father's will. Aimee closed her eyes very tight while Robert prayed. She saw the room filled with angels who lined a golden pathway reaching into the future and she and Robert walking hand in hand. When she opened her eyes the picture faded, but when she closed her eyes again there was only one figure, she alone. She did not understand the meaning of the picture then, but she whispered "yes" to Robert and in her heart "yes" to God, little realizing the full implications.

Robert Semple married
Aimee in 1908.

Wedding Bells

Once it was decided that Aimee and Robert were going
to be married, plans began to take shape for a grand wedding
at Kozy Kot farm. On August 12, 1908, they were married
on the lawn by Lt. Col. John D. Sharpe of the London
Salvation Army Corps. As the happy couple stood under a
bower of cedar and pine covered with golden flowers,
Robert placed the ring on Aimee's finger.

Then the guests sat down to a splendid meal catered by
Brooks Brothers of Ingersoll, after which the happy couple
rode off in a carriage to the railway station. They then went
by train to Toronto for a brief honeymoon before settling in
Stratford, Ontario, the site of Robert's pastorate.

4. Pastoring and Itinerating

Robert Semple was of Irish-Scottish parentage from the town of Magherafelt, near Belfast, Northern Ireland. He had come into contact with the Pentecostals through two early missions, the North Avenue in Chicago and the Hebdens' East End Mission in Toronto. It was from the Toronto mission that Semple went to minister in Ingersoll and Stratford. He was the speaker in the Ingersoll mission when Aimee Kennedy and her father, James, had dropped in to observe.

Stratford, Ontario

John Wietersen, a Stratford merchant, assisted by his brother Charles, was in charge of the Union Mission in Stratford when it was opened on April 7, 1907. The first speaker was Herbert Randall, a returned missionary from Egypt who had received the Holy Spirit baptism at the Hebden Mission. It was he who opened the Pentecostal church in Ingersoll in October 1907.

Robert and Aimee's First Church

After their honeymoon, Aimee joined Robert in the pastorate at Stratford. A recent picture of the meeting hall is shown in this chapter. It is a yellow brick building at 20 Erie Street. Apart from the windows, the outward appearance of the building is probably much the same as it was 100 years ago. A long, narrow stairway of about twenty-five steps leads from street level to the hall's location on the second floor.

No longer an auditorium, the second story has a corridor running down the middle with small rooms on either side. The outside view shows the high, narrow window frames of the original hall now bricked in to room-size windows. What a contrast this was to the magnificent Angelus Temple, which would eventually be Aimee's church in Los Angeles!

The upper floor of 20 Erie Street in Stratford, Ontario, housed the Union Mission.

Oldest Artifact: Little Black Book

A small black book used by Charles Wietersen, the Stratford mission's first secretary, lists small purchases, such as chairs, coal oil and offerings, from April 1907. This booklet, now in the Pentecostal Assemblies of Canada (PAOC) archives in Mississauga, Ontario, is the oldest known Pentecostal artifact in Canada.

Living Quarters

The Semples resided on Falstaff Street. Robert worked in the sprawling railway locomotive shops that dominated that part of the city. Aimee, a dutiful young wife, washed their laundry and hung it out to dry, as she would have done back home on the farm. To her dismay, she found her white sheets covered with soot that drifted over the city from the smokestacks!

Second Meeting Place

At some point in its early history, the Stratford congregation moved to a large, attractive red brick house at 18 Brunswick Street. Today it houses a dental office.

In the early 1900s, this property at 18 Brunswick St. in Stratford, Ontario, served as the area's Pentecostal meeting place.

London, Ontario

Towards the end of 1908 the Semples left Stratford for Chicago. On the way, they stopped for several weeks of meetings in the city of London, Ontario, where Pentecostal house meetings were already being conducted. The meeting house belonged to a Mr. and Mrs. Armstrong. It was here that the Semples lived and ministered. After several weeks of ministry in London they moved on to Chicago.

Chicago, Illinois

There may have been several reasons for the couple's sojourn in Chicago. The North Avenue Mission was a thriving hub for Pentecostals living in the area and for those passing through. William Durham, the highly respected pastor, was a man of the Spirit, and the Semples could gain much valuable experience by working with him. His mission, in turn, would benefit from this pair of talented and willing young workers. Then too, the Semples were bound for the mission field in China and could benefit from both the prayers and financial backing of an established church such as this one in Chicago. While there, Robert and Aimee were ordained by Durham. This gave them some semblance of official recognition, helpful in their travels abroad.

Findlay, Ohio

In October 1909, the Semples joined Durham for two weeks of meetings in Thomas K. Leonard's church and Bible school in Findlay, Ohio. Protracted meetings such as this provided a wonderful opportunity for God's people to join in united prayer and heart searching. Many were filled with the Spirit.

One time when Aimee was hurrying downstairs to join in prayer she slipped and fell. Her ankle was badly dislocated and began to swell. A couple of medical doctors attended to her. The bone in her foot was cracked. It had been wrenched backward in the fall, severing the ligaments that moved her toes. Aimee said she was suffering such excruciating pain that she could not concentrate on faith for healing. When the swelling was reduced sufficiently, her foot was placed in a plaster of paris cast. She used a pair of crutches to hobble to the train that took them back to Chicago.

A Healing Miracle

In Chicago, Aimee felt God leading her to ask for prayer for healing. It seemed like a voice spoke to her, saying, "*If you will wrap up the shoe from your broken foot and go over to the North Avenue Mission to Brother Durham and ask him to lay hands on your foot, I will heal it.*" At first she laughed at the thought, but the voice impressed her to obey. People began to pray. Pastor Durham was in prayer, walking up and down in the room, when suddenly he stopped and laid his hands upon her ankle, calling out, "*In the name of Jesus, receive your healing.*" Immediately, the pain left.

Walking, and Leaping, and Praising God

It was like the healing of the man at the beautiful gate of the temple in Acts, chapter 3. When the cast was removed, she put on her stocking and shoe and leaped to her feet with joy. This was Aimee's first personal healing and it gave her faith to believe for the healing of others.

Back to Canada

Early in 1910, Robert and Aimee realized they should get ready for the first leg of their long journey to China. Durham accompanied them as they held meetings on the way. First it was a stop in Kitchener, where a Pentecostal convention was in progress, then to London, Ontario. The meetings in London had outgrown the Armstrong home and were now held in the spacious residence of Methodist layman W. H. Wortman, a wealthy manufacturer, who opened both home and heart to the moving of the Holy Spirit. In 1921, his son, Dr. Charles Wortman, a specialist in obstetrics from Bellevue Hospital, New York, served as a Pentecostal missionary in Argentina. In 1939, he returned to Canada to fill the position of General Secretary of the Pentecostal Assemblies of Canada.

The mission at London was ready for another wave of refreshing when the Semples and Durham arrived in 1910. When they left three weeks later, thirty believers had received the baptism in the Holy Spirit.

Resuming their travels, the Semples were able to stop over at Ingersoll and Salford and bid farewell to loved ones.

Toronto

Then it was on to Toronto for the final send-off. Another Pentecostal convention was in progress when they arrived at the Hebden Mission. The Semples spent ten happy days there before departing for overseas. A crowd gathered at Union Station to bid the last farewell, with the familiar words of "God be with you till we meet again." Little did they realize that Robert Semple would never return.

5. En Route to Hong Kong

Robert and Aimee sailed from Saint John, New Brunswick, on their way to Liverpool and Robert's family home in Ireland. In Belfast they found a hospitable group of new Pentecostal believers that had been established since Robert had left home some years before. Knowing that Aimee was expecting her first child, family and friends sent them off with an additional trunk full of clothes and gifts.

London's Royal Albert Hall

Canadian friends advised the Semples to stop in London, England, and call upon Cecil Polhill, the well-known Christian millionaire. It seems that missionaries were often accommodated at Mr. Polhill's home, as were the Semples. A uniformed butler greeted them and a gold-braided doorman took their luggage. Mr. Polhill himself graciously received them in his library and then they were shown to their room.

There was to be a meeting in Royal Albert Hall later that day. The hall had been opened in 1871 and dedicated to Queen Victoria's husband, Prince Albert. Its oval shape has a seating capacity of 8,000, although it has accommodated up to 12,000. Tier upon tier of seats rise toward the 135-foot dome.

Periodically, evangelical Christians have occupied the facilities for special conventions. One such convention was in progress when the Semples arrived. Robert was engaged in business meetings throughout the day, probably involving their mission to China, while Aimee remained in the room. Her host informed her that she was expected to take her turn speaking, but Aimee felt intimidated and tried in vain to decline. Though she searched her Bible diligently, she was at a loss for a message.

Finally, the driver told her they were late and she must come. She was surprised at the size of the building but assumed that her meeting would be in a small room.

Suddenly, a stage door opened and she was thrust unto the platform. Thousands of people sat in tiers up to the fifth balcony. Aimee was petrified. Without hesitation, the leader introduced her. Closing her eyes, she prayed through chattering teeth for God to help.

Royal Albert Hall at night. En route to China in 1910, Aimee Semple addressed a large assembly at one of England's most treasured and distinctive auditoriums.

A Prophetic Message

Her Bible fell open at Joel 1:4 and suddenly the power of the Holy Spirit came upon her and words began to flow from her lips. This time it was in English, not in another language. She heard herself speaking fluently as people leaned forward in their seats to catch her every word. It was a masterful message describing the dispensation of the Holy Spirit. She explained how the palmerworm and locusts had gone though the land destroying the crops, but God came to restore the damage and pour out His Spirit in revival.

Prophetically, she was describing the initial outpouring of the Holy Spirit on the Day of Pentecost, with the accompanying signs, wonders and response. This, she explained, continued for a while, but little by little the church began to compromise.

It lost its first love and its zeal diminished. Aimee painted a picture of the Dark Ages when the spiritual flame burned low. Then she brought them through the reformation and subsequent revivals to the 20th century outpouring of the Holy Spirit. It was a very unusual message and well received.

Hong Kong

Soon they were on their way again as friends gathered at the wharf to sing "God Will Take Care Of You." They enjoyed the long ocean voyage as Robert studied the Bible for hours and shared his thoughts with Aimee. At a number of ports they met members of the growing Pentecostal family, who encouraged them on their way.

After weathering a typhoon, the sky cleared and they glimpsed the mountain of Hong Kong in the early morning sunrise. They were met by other missionaries, including Phoebe Holmes of Michigan, sent out a month earlier by Durham's church in Chicago. The Semples and Phoebe rented two large rooms with a kitchen and bath at the back. They engaged a Chinese teacher and soon settled in to learn the language together. They discovered that they could live economically by buying bread, oats, rice, potatoes, vegetables, steak and butter. They bought milk in cans, which, incidentally, came from the Borden plant away back in Ingersoll, Canada!

Robert did not waste any time. He began preaching through an interpreter and distributing Christian literature. The three of them spent hours in prayer for the harvest field before them. They must not have realized that they needed to take special precautions to protect themselves from sickness and disease. They bought fresh food from the market, ate it without proper sterilization and drank water that had a strange taste. After a few weeks Robert showed signs of dysentery. While visiting Macau a month later, both of the Semples came down with malaria. They were taken back to Hong Kong and placed in a mountaintop facility operated by the English for those unable to afford care. Robert and Aimee were separated in the men's and women's wards with only brief visits allowed when Aimee was able to walk to the other building. Their situation looked bleak. Robert was weakening and Aimee was eight months pregnant.

6. Death and Desolation

On their second wedding anniversary, August 12, 1910, they were only able to exchange notes. A week later, Aimee was given permission for a very short visit. Unknown to her it was to be their last. Robert told her he knew he was going to be with Jesus. As the nurse escorted Aimee away the last words Robert spoke were, "*Good night dear; I'll see you in the morning.*" Later that same night Aimee was called to Robert's bedside with these words, "*Come quickly! He is sinking fast.*" He was unconscious. As she held his hand, his spirit slipped away at 1:00 a.m. Aimee was only twenty years of age and had never before seen anyone die. Added to that, Robert had not lived to see their baby.

Alone, and on the other side of the world from home and loved ones, Aimee sank down by Robert's bedside, clinging to his cold hand. She had never dreamed of them parting, but it was true. Then, just at her lowest point, the Comforter, God's Holy Spirit, enabled her to say, "*Glory to Jesus! The Lord gave and the Lord taketh away. Blessed be the name of the Lord!*" (See Job 1:21.)

Then she felt the doctor shaking her by the shoulder, as the Lord spoke into her ears, "*He is not here; he is risen.*" (See Luke 24:36.) God wrapped His strong arms of love about her, reassuring her.

So Much to Face

What would she do? The oriental custom required a quick burial, but she had only five dollars and thirty cents. Just then the mailman came by. "*Letter for you, Mrs. Semple.*"

Listlessly, she opened the envelope and several bills of American currency fluttered out. There was sixty-five dollars. *"Enough for a coffin,"* she whispered, *"and maybe enough for a grave."* The letter was from Chicago, and it read:

> *Greetings in the precious name of Jesus! What is wrong? The Lord wakened my sister and me in the middle of the night and bade us send you this money. At first we demurred, thinking to rise in the morning and secure a money order, but the Lord assured us of its safe arrival (cash in the mail). I dressed hurriedly and will make my way to the nearest mailbox. But please do tell us why this urgent need.*[3]

All Alone

Few can understand the depths of sorrow that Aimee experienced and the unanswered questions that ran through her mind. Why had Robert been taken from her and his calling? What should she do next? Which way should she turn? Morning after morning she would awake with a scream as the reality of her great loss dawned upon her.

From our present viewpoint we can see the future times of glorious blessings and power that were to come upon Aimee and her ministry. All of that was unknown to her way back there. Were these severe trials a part of God's training for the future? She had no idea what God had in store for her, but when He had tried her faith it came forth more precious than gold tried in the fire (1 Peter 1:7).

Immediate Decisions

The coffin and burial had to be taken care of. Arrangements were made for interment in Hong Kong's beautiful Happy Valley Cemetery. Aimee was not able to go to the cemetery. It was a sad procession of missionaries that made its way through the streets to the graveside. Thoughts rushed through their troubled minds. Why was one of their most promising recruits snatched by death? Why was his young widow left to sorrow alone in a land so far from home and loved ones?

Roberta's Birth

A month after Robert died, little Roberta was born and named in her father's memory. But she was weak and sickly. Aimee wanted to stay on and fulfill her ministry in China, but others advised against it. They said that if she stayed Roberta would have only a small chance of surviving.

Return Voyage

Aimee's mother, Minnie, sent funds to cover the return fare. When Roberta was six weeks old they sailed for San Francisco. Other passengers looked on with curiosity as they saw the young widow with a tiny infant, traveling alone. But when they found out she was a missionary widow they insisted that she conduct a Sunday service on board. Aimee did not attempt to preach but played the piano, led them in singing hymns, read the Bible a bit and cried a bit. Each Sunday, the salon was crowded with people looking in the windows. The captain said he had never before seen such attention.

Arriving in America

When she disembarked, the purser placed an envelope in her hand. It contained sixty-seven dollars from the passengers, enough to help her reach New York and relatives. Rather than going to the Kennedy home at Ingersoll, Aimee's destination was New York City, where her mother, Minnie, had gone to work at the Salvation Army headquarters. Evangeline Booth had moved from the office of Army Commissioner in Canada to Commissioner in the United States in 1904. She had taken several staff members with her. Minnie knew some of these and felt right at home in the big city.

7. Adrift

"Adrift" best describes Aimee's life in this period of time. Her call to the ministry and marriage to Robert Semple had taken her to lofty heights and halfway around the world. Then, suddenly, the one she held so dear was snatched from her. She had no husband, but did she still have the call? If so, what could she do about it? If not, then her call to ministry was no longer valid. What should she do?

Meanwhile, as she tried to sort out all these things, she and Roberta shared an apartment with Minnie near the Army headquarters in New York. Minnie's duties involved fundraising, volunteers and collecting money in a designated area of the city. She was given the title of "Envoy." Within a week of Aimee's arrival, Minnie had borrowed a uniform for Aimee and put her to work serving lunch at a midtown rescue mission. On Sundays, Minnie and Aimee attended services at the Army barracks. Sometimes Aimee, longing for old times, attended Glad Tidings Pentecostal Assembly, pastored by Robert and Marie (Burgess) Brown. But she was restless. She visited Chicago twice or more, wondering if a niche for ministry would open there, but it did not develop. She went home to her father, James Kennedy, at Salford, but no door of service opened. Roberta was too weak and frail for Aimee to take with her as she ministered. The doctor advised her to settle down and devote herself to the care of her child.

Harold McPherson

Aimee returned to her work in New York City with the Army and somehow became acquainted with Harold

McPherson, a decent, friendly young man. He was the cashier in a fashionable downtown restaurant. Concerned for Aimee's safety after work, he waited late each night to accompany her home. Perhaps their mutual loneliness drew them together. Their friendship grew as Harold accompanied her on the nightly subway ride. Then they began attending various events together. Could Harold be the answer to her restlessness? He was willing to take both Aimee and Roberta and provide them a comfortable home, but Minnie did not approve. She thought Harold was a nice person, but his lack of strong religious convictions concerned her. Harold, however, did have a religious background. He was born in Providence, Rhode Island, in 1890, the same year as Aimee. His father, William McPherson, came from a family of Nova Scotia fishermen. Harold had professed conversion to Christ during a Gipsy Smith meeting in Providence in 1907 and even felt a call to the ministry. He entered William Jewel College to prepare but had to drop out when his mother took sick and needed his help.

Proposal

When Harold proposed, Aimee saw it as a chance to settle down in a home of her own. Harold and Aimee both felt they would be more free away from Minnie's influence, so in February 1912, they eloped to Chicago! Aimee had friends there and soon became happily involved in church life, so much so that Harold thought she was putting her friends and church before him. He felt he had to get her away from the people who had known her as the wife of Robert Semple. The answer seemed to be another move. Harold decided on going to Providence in the hope that his mother's influence and example as a homemaker would be a good role model for Aimee. In the meantime they had become reconciled with Minnie, who accepted their marriage.

A Home of Their Own

They went about furnishing a new place of their own in Providence with carpets, curtains and brass beds. On March 23, 1913, their son, Rolf, was born. When he was only a few weeks old he reached up his little hand and began to pat Aimee's face. Later, she said, "*Not one moment since he was born has he ever caused me a tear, or a heartache, or an embarrassment of any kind.*" He was to be her most consistent and loyal friend.

Like Jonah

Aimee, in reality, became like Jonah, the runaway prophet. In her effort to get away from the call to Christian ministry and settle down in a comfortable, domestic lifestyle she was stifling the voice of the Holy Spirit. She said,

> *I became lukewarm, then cold in my experience, discovered that there is no such thing as standing still. I was going backward (drifting). The pleasures and cares of this world came crowding in till I discovered I was losing my first love. Then came sickness. Inside of one year I underwent two serious operations. It seemed there was not a sound part left in my body. I had no chance to enjoy my comfortable home, except what little I could see from my pillow.*
>
> *For a year I grew weaker and weaker. At times it seemed I would lose my reason. The hand of God was heavy upon me, and His voice rang continually in my ears, "Now will you go and preach the Word?" When I prayed for deliverance, the only answer I received was, "Now will you go?" At last, when taken off the operating table more dead than alive, I answered the call*

and said, "Yes, Lord; I'll go." From that moment I
began to improve, and in a few weeks was up and well.[4]

Stepping Out Alone

Aimee was unable to argue the point with Harold or his mother. They had never seen or heard her minister and would not countenance such a thought. To Aimee it was either "go" or "die," so she packed her suitcase and with her two babies took a taxi to the railway station and headed for her old home in Canada. Minnie was back home at the time. She and James met them at the station and drove them home. If Aimee was to attempt full-time ministry, Minnie was the key, because she could care for the children. Minnie informed Aimee that there was a camp meeting in progress in Berlin (Kitchener, Ontario) and she could attend while they minded the children—just what Aimee needed!

Kitchener Camp Meeting—1915

Early the next morning before she boarded the train for the camp, Aimee sent a telegram to Harold, telling him where she was and what she was doing. Aimee arrived at the camp and joined the seekers. As she tearfully pleaded with God to forgive her for wandering from His will, she suddenly felt the loving presence of a forgiving God and soon began to help others seeking at the altar.

By the end of the Kitchener camp meeting Aimee had two invitations to minister. She accepted both of them. One was to help at a camp to begin shortly in London, Ontario, and the other was from Mrs. Elizabeth Sharpe, asking Aimee to come to Mount Forest, Ontario, and conduct evangelistic meetings in her mission.

London Camp Meeting—1915

Aimee and Robert had ministered in London before going to China. At the close of the Kitchener camp, Aimee returned to the farm at Salford. All seemed to be going well. James and Minnie were happy to have them home on the farm.

Part of Aimee's task was to make a twenty-five foot sign to hang across the street in London. She and James worked hard to get it ready on time. The Holy Spirit anointed her in the London meetings, as He did in Kitchener, and Aimee was assured that she was on the right pathway. Even though letters kept coming from Harold urging her to return, the call of God must come first. She dare not turn back.

8. Mount Forest: The Turning Point

A Beautiful Small Town—1915

Mount Forest has the distinction of being the highest point above sea level in southern Ontario, as shown by the current photo of its water tower. Initially it appeared that Aimee's meetings were doomed to failure due to lack of interest. The mission was a small building on the main street with only fifty chairs. Aimee soon discovered that the same few people sat in those seats at each meeting. Most of the townsfolk paid no attention, and it looked like it was going to be the end of her most recent venture into full-time ministry. Then, a very simple act helped turn the tide.

The following quote from Mrs. McPherson describes what she did.

A Chair on Main Street

I surveyed the scene and sought to lay my plans for a siege of souls. The sleepy little town lazed in the sunset.

How could I gain their attention? I remembered Robert Semple's slogan: "When in doubt, pray." So, I started in. Setting my chair down firmly just outside the curb, I mounted my tiny rostrum, lifted my hands high to heaven, closed my eyes, and just stood there lifting my heart to God without speaking a single word aloud. Minutes passed. Nothing happened, but I never moved, never spoke, never lowered my arms.

Then a wave of interest and excitement stirred the

populace. Footsteps hurried from all directions until a sizable crowd had gathered, but I never moved. I was afraid to by now. One would not have realized that there were so many people on the street!

I Opened My Eyes and Looked Wildly Around.

Then I began to tremble. But though I tried to speak, not a word would come. My mouth merely opened and closed several times. Then with desperation, I shouted, "People—follow me, quick!" Jumping down off the chair, I hooked my arm through its back and ran off up the street toward the mission. The crowd ran after me. I never stopped till I reached the door. I ran in and, they ran in too. Racing to the little platform...

I Cried to The Doorkeeper,

"Lock that door and keep it locked till I get through!" Having gotten the people, I was fearful lest I could not hold their interest. But they showed no inclination to leave. That practically settled the crowd problem. I have never had to seriously worry over it since that eventful day. If you are annoyed over attendance, why not try the chair-and-prayer method at some busy intersection? I can heartily recommend it and practically guarantee that it will work. Anyway, I preached to those people for forty minutes.

The next night there were as many outside the hall as were able to get into it. "It is a lovely evening. Why not try preaching outside on the lawn?" someone suggested. The crowd trooped out and sat on the grass while I preached on the piazza. The piano was hastily trundled out, and some farmers removed the lanterns from their wagons and tied them in the trees.

And So I Had a Great Church After All.

My dome was the starry heavens. For music, the wind whispered through the pines. For pews, we had the soft, green velvet of the lawn. For parishioners, there were men in denim overalls and women in alpaca housedresses. For a penitent form, we utilized the crumbling edge of the piazza. It was all very thrilling!

Great broad-shouldered farmers came down to the improvised altar and gave their hearts to the Lord. All that week I preached out-of-doors, scores wept their way into the Kingdom. The crowd grew in numbers till we had more than five hundred. They arrived on horseback, on bicycles, in buggies and wagons. They arrived on foot and they arrived in new horseless carriages.[5]

In 1915, residents of Mount Forest, Ontario, northwest of Toronto, responded to the young evangelist's bold call to sinners.

The Town Crier

There was a man they called "The Town Crier" who walked up and down the main street ringing his bell and calling out news about the theater, ball games and whatever. Everybody knew him. He was suffering from a physical affliction that had plagued him for about a year. But now, God miraculously healed him and soon he was the talk of the town. Talk about good publicity. That was it! The doctor, his old bar mates—everybody knew about it. Crowds overflowed onto the lawn. People were saved, healed and baptized in the Spirit.

A Tent

Aimee was able to purchase a used tent, but when it was unfolded they found it had holes and mildew. Not to be deterred, other women rallied to Aimee's side and together they patched and mended until it became usable.

Harold McPherson Arrives

In the midst of all this, Aimee's husband, Harold, caught up with her. In awe, he witnessed the meetings in full swing. For the first time he saw her ministry in action. He was impressed and joined others at the altar in prayer and surrender. When the meetings were over, they both went back to the farm at Ingersoll to share the good news with family.

9. A Fresh Start

Things had changed. Harold was now willing to join Aimee in her work, so they took Rolf with them to Providence and left Roberta on the farm, to the delight of her grandparents. Harold and Aimee closed down their home in Providence and joined the ranks of itinerant evangelists on the "Sawdust Trail." They ordered a new 40 x 80 foot tent in preparation for meetings in the summer of 1916. Until then, they engaged in services in any mission that was open for meetings.

They planned to set up their new tent in Providence first, but it was not ready in time, so the company shipped a used tent in its place. Not being used to selecting a proper site, Aimee chose to pitch it in a very visible hilltop spot, which turned out also to be very vulnerable. One morning before the end of the meetings they found that the winds had torn the tent beyond repair.

By that time, Harold had gone back to secular employment and was not there to help. Meanwhile, Aimee found a boy to assist her and they set about solving the problem. They gathered up smaller tents, fastened them together to form a makeshift shelter and had it ready for the service.

Framingham

Aimee's next move was to an excellent location on an old campground at Framingham, Massachusetts. Pentecostals from across the northeast flocked to the services. The meetings went well, although Harold continued to waiver. About that time he had three dreams in which he was told to go back and help his wife with the tents, so when Aimee left Framingham Harold was with her. It was now the fall of 1916 and they shipped the tent to Florida for the winter months. On one such trip Harold considered it the happiest of his marriage. When he closed each tent site, he took pride in leaving the property in better shape than he had found it.

A rolling billboard. The Gospel Car enabled more meeting sites per day and provided a means of distributing literature. Harold McPherson is at the wheel.

The Atlantic Seaboard

For two years, Aimee crisscrossed the Atlantic seaboard, north and south: summer in the north and winter in the south. It was a pattern that drew the crowds in both seasons, and Aimee's meetings were becoming better known with larger attendance. She preached in Boston, Onset Bay, Long Island, New York, Savannah, Jacksonville, Tampa, St. Petersburg, Orlando, Palm Beach, Miami, Key West and other points. Black and white people generally attended the same services and Aimee ministered to all alike.

The Printed Message

Aimee made great use of the printed word, distributing Christian literature far and wide. In June of 1917, she began her publication called *The Bridal Call*. Her life story, *This Is That*, came off the press over two years later, in October 1919.

10. No Turning Back

Finally, Harold became tired of the transient lifestyle and made his decision not to spend the rest of his life roaming from one tent location to another. After much debate, Aimee went her way and Harold returned to the business world. Aimee felt bound by God to be faithful to her call. If only they could have foreseen the future, things might have worked out better.

When Aimee later opened her mega church in Los Angeles her ministry had a home base where she spent a great deal of time. Had Harold been with her, he could have shared in business details and lifted the burden from Aimee's and Minnie's shoulders. It might have helped both of them and saved their marriage, but it did not turn out that way. There is a tendency to blame Aimee entirely for the separation, but from her standpoint she felt she must obey God in full-time service. She believed that her actions were justified. They divorced quietly. They did not quarrel, but they both recognized their marriage was not working.

National Camp Meeting, Philadelphia—1918

This was Aimee's biggest undertaking up to that time. The plan was conceived a year before. Philadelphia was a strategic location with access to a very large population. If the crowd doubled or tripled the usual numbers, it meant she was reaching many more people simultaneously. She prayed for a tent big enough to hold the expected crowds and found just the one she needed in Philadelphia. It had been ordered by another party who was not able to take delivery.

A local committee had set up a tent city capable of accommodating large crowds. The site was ideal, a campground, with a space for the big top (meeting tent) surrounded by rows of smaller tents for sleeping, dining and so on. Aimee was left free to concentrate her efforts on the services. It was the ideal setup, conducive for maximum results. The meetings lasted for six weeks, with good outcome in spite of some opposition.

11. Coast to Coast

Prior to heading west, Aimee toured the New England states, preaching as she went. She closed her New York City services in mid-fall and prepared to go west. Then, a couple of things happened that would have discouraged those of lesser faith. It was at the height of the 1918 influenza epidemic, when public meetings were greatly curtailed. A Presbyterian minister, turned Pentecostal, had invited Aimee to stop and speak at his large church in Tulsa, Oklahoma. Now, he wired and said not to come, because all the churches had been shut down. But Aimee, convinced that God was leading her west, ignored the warnings and started out. Again, she was vindicated, because by the time she reached Tulsa the ban had been lifted.

Finally—Westward Ho!

Aimee visualized both the need and the potential for ministering to the masses that were migrating westward, and she was right. She sold the old car and Minnie paid the difference so Aimee could buy a new Oldsmobile for the trip west. Aimee drove all the way. She may have been the first woman to drive across the continent without the help of a man. It was a bold act of faith, and she took that step, where others may have hesitated.

Mile upon Mile, Day after Day

It must have seemed like an endless journey for the four of them, Aimee, Minnie and the two children. Would they ever be able to settle down like most people and live in a house of their own? God impressed upon Aimee that He would provide a bungalow for them in Los Angeles and she told the children the same. There were no transcontinental freeways in those days. Aimee wrote these words about the trip:

> *On this first tour, notwithstanding the fact that it was undertaken long before cross-continental motoring became popular, I drove virtually all the way myself, driving frequently two hundred miles a day over uncharted, unpaved roads, holding services in the evening and then going on again. Thousands of tracts and pieces of Gospel literature were given out en route* (The Personal Testimony of Aimee Semple McPherson, 47).

Necessary Provisions

They turned what might have been a difficult journey into an adventure for God. Their gear was carried in the trunk, with extra water and fuel stacked on the running boards. Each night they stopped to pitch their tent, cook their meal and set up their cots. They drew water for washing and cooking from some nearby spring or brook. When feasible, travel was in convoy with other motorists for safety's sake.

On the road, a good meal could depend upon one's resourcefulness.

12. City of Angels

One day in mid-December 1918, after months of travel, their automobile broke over the last crest of mountains and glided down into Los Angeles, the City of Angels. The angels of heaven must have looked down and rejoiced in anticipation of the copious showers of blessings that were about to fall upon that city and America's west coast.

Beyond Azusa Street

The Azusa Mission and other Pentecostal groups had witnessed an initial outpouring of the Holy Spirit early in the twentieth century, but now the Pentecostal revival was about to overflow the small storefront missions and reach thousands and thousands in the world beyond.

Emerging Leaders—A Product of the Revival

Others have noted that many prominent leaders in the Pentecostal revival were themselves a product of that revival. This is borne out in the fact that not until the 1920s did mass meetings or extensive missionary efforts become more common and they were often led by those who were products of the Pentecostal revival. Mrs. Semple and Dr. Charles Price are examples.

Preaching in Los Angeles

Mrs. McPherson described how after her arrival she got right to the work of ministering in the city:

Just two days after we arrived we began a revival. Our first meetings were held in an upstairs hall; our second in a church. The Lord poured out His Spirit in copious showers from on high. The buildings soon grew too small and Clunes Auditorium, seating 3,500, was engaged for the larger meetings.[6]

"Excuse Me, Please"

One evening just before Aimee rose to speak, a young woman stood to her feet in the audience. She spoke out, saying that she had four lots of land and felt the Lord wanted her to give one lot to Mrs. McPherson to build a bungalow for her family. Then a man spoke out that he would dig the basement. Soon other voices joined in, offering to help with other parts of the house and furnishings. In just three months the house was up and furnished, and they moved in with a housekeeper who cared for the children and the household, leaving Aimee free to minister in the city and beyond. When the church in Los Angeles became established, Aimee carried the ministry role. Minnie was busily engaged with the administration end of the work and others took their respective places.

Why the Ready Response in Los Angeles?

Dr. Edith Blumhofer answers this question as follows:

Why did these Angelenos so readily embrace Aimee, spend their money and their time to provide for her and want an ongoing part in her efforts? Los Angeles Pentecostals apparently found Aimee a refreshing change from the shifting group of men who had come and gone in Los Angeles's Pentecostal missions since 1906.[7]

13. Great Multitudes—1919

From this point onward readers will observe changes taking place in the direction of Aimee's ministry. Her home was established in the city of Los Angeles. This was now the base from which she operated, going first to the city itself, then to other cities of North America and overseas.

In Aimee's numerous country-wide tours, prior to establishing Angelus Temple, meetings were conducted in some of the largest auditoriums, ranging in capacity from 3,000 to 16,000. The primary purpose was to win souls to Christ, but wherever she ministered across the continent, people gave willingly toward the establishment of a home church in Los Angeles. Only in that way could she garner resources capable of such an undertaking.

Beholding God in Action

Not every meeting is covered in detail, but many highlights and faith-building stories are reported. You will be stirred by many miraculous events that took place during this time in Mrs. McPherson's ministry. Even hardened reporters were often awed by what they witnessed. These events are recorded that God might be glorified and His handmaiden given credibility.

San Francisco—1919

In February, Aimee left Los Angeles in response to an invitation from Pastor and Mrs. Robert Craig of Glad Tidings

Temple in San Francisco. Craig was a Canadian Methodist minister in frail health who had gone to California, perhaps in search of a more healthful climate. In July of 1911, he was invited to attend a Pentecostal mission in Los Angeles. Within a few days his whole life was changed.

He was baptized in the Holy Spirit and made well in body. His new energy was channeled into a very productive ministry as he established Pentecostal meetings in downtown San Francisco. By the year 1915 his meetings were held in a large hall on Ellis Street, and by 1919 he was in the process of opening a Bible school. The Craigs' work continued to prosper in the surrounding area and later became the basis of the Northern California-Nevada District of the Assemblies of God.

An Assemblies of God Evangelist

It was Craig who encouraged Aimee to take out ministerial papers with the Assemblies of God and in April 1919 she became affiliated with the Assemblies for a period of about three years.

Sometimes a ministry becomes so large that it is difficult to accommodate within an existing denomination. Mrs. McPherson's church and followers eventually formed their own organization, the International Church of the Foursquare Gospel. However, they enjoy close fellowship with the Assemblies of God and other Pentecostal bodies.

Many Meetings

Aimee continued to minister in California: San Francisco, San Jose and Los Angeles. Then Tulsa beckoned for meetings again in April 1919. Large numbers came from afar seeking healing.

Most of June was spent in Chicago with overflow crowds. Next, it was east into Pennsylvania and back to New York City for a month of meetings in a tent pitched right in the Bronx. Troublemakers, as is often the case, unwittingly drew the curious, which in turn extended the outreach. It was a great beacon light in the darkness to show the way of salvation.

Los Angeles Tent Meetings

In August 1919, Aimee drove back to Los Angeles for tent meetings with the west coast Pentecostals. They had staked out a nine-acre lot with tents for meetings, dining and sleeping. The big tent had a fifty-foot platform crowded each evening with participants, singers and musicians. Smaller meetings were held in the daytime, while large crowds swarmed into the big top each evening to hear Aimee speak. She was only twenty-nine years of age at the time, but she commanded the respect of both preachers and lay people alike. Altars were filled with seekers night after night. Could it be that the soul travail of Azusa was now bearing fruit in these glorious meetings?

Holdrege, Akron, Baltimore

Aimee spent the fall of 1919 in meetings in Holdrege, Nebraska, and in the 2,500-seat armory in Akron, Ohio. She blazed a trail of evangelism wherever she went. In December she was in Baltimore for seventeen days, where they rented the spacious Lyric Theater for $300 per day.

Order or Disorder?

It was in Baltimore that Sister (as Aimee was often respectfully addressed) piloted her meetings around the rocks of fanaticism. The tremendous influx of Holy Spirit power that came upon seekers in the early 1900s was new to preachers and the people alike. They meant so well with their newfound exuberance and joy, but they sometimes did not stop to distinguish the difference between the presence of the Holy Spirit and the joy and excitement that often come at the same time. It is not proper to deliberately generate excitement in an effort to bring the Holy Spirit. It ought to be the other way around. Seek His presence, exalt Him and He will "show up," bringing His joy and peace with Him. "*Draw near to God and He will draw near to you*" (James 4:8).

When the Pharisees asked Jesus to silence His followers, He said to them, "*I tell you that if these should keep silent, the stones would immediately cry out*" (Luke 19:40). God is not the author of confusion. There is a time for vocal praise and a time to be silent.

Upon return from a speaking engagement, the cheerful faces of Roberta and Rolf provided Aimee with a warm welcome home.

14. Ring the Bells of Heaven—1920

There is Joy Today!

After Aimee spent Christmas holidays with her family in their Los Angeles home, it was back to Baltimore and meetings in a number of other churches. Dr. Charles A. Shreve, pastor of the McKendree Methodist Episcopal Church in Washington, D.C., attended the Baltimore meetings with his church board. They liked what they saw and pled with Mrs. McPherson to come to their church. She promised, but first there was another engagement to fulfill.

Winnipeg, Manitoba

Winnipeg was the site of the earliest Pentecostal meetings in western Canada under the sponsorship of A. H. Argue. By 1920, the congregation consisted of a good nucleus of Pentecostal believers who had purchased the old Wesley Methodist Church, seating 1,700.

Aimee Semple McPherson Arrives

Aimee opened a campaign there on February 15, 1920. As she alighted from the train and rode to the hotel in a horse-drawn cutter, she began to think of how to gain the attention of the worldly-minded masses. True to form, she came up with a plan that had never been tried in Winnipeg. She determined to go and visit the red light district, pool rooms and dance halls. When the chief of police learned of this, he volunteered to escort her.

The Lady in White

One Saturday night in February 1920, 2,000 dancers in the Alhambra night club were surprised when the manager stopped them and introduced a vibrant lady dressed all in white. Her appearance and mission must have startled them. The orchestra, being forewarned, struck up a favorite hymn. Aimee led in the chorus and gave a five-minute talk, not of condemnation but warm greetings from one who cared.

After distributing tracts and Bibles, she announced her meetings at Wesley Church. When she asked for a show of hands from those who promised to attend her meetings, there was a good response. This same procedure was repeated that night in various places of worldly entertainment. She would often stop and speak a word with the patrons.

An Amazing Response

Next morning, the 1,700-seat church was filled to capacity. People were packed into the auditorium, the stairways, the basement, and still there were throngs outside. She had caught the attention of the city. The altar services were filled with hungry seekers and miracles of healing took place. Before she left Winnipeg many had found Christ as Savior and the Pentecostal congregation was considerably larger.

Baltimore and Washington

Back on the east coast, Aimee stopped briefly in Baltimore to conclude her series of meetings there, and then she was on to Washington, D.C., to the two-thousand-seat McKendree Methodist Episcopal Church. According to an April 29, 1920, report in the *Methodist*, "*Mrs. McPherson preached the Gospel in power and demonstration of the Spirit,*

*exhibiting a beautiful combination of faith and love and spir-
itual understanding of the Word of God."*

Many thronged the services for healing. One day Mrs.
McPherson and Pastor Shreve prayed for 800 sick folk.
Though it was organized as a local church meeting rather
than a city-wide campaign, some considered it to be the cap-
ital's most stirring religious event up to that time.[8]

Lethbridge, Alberta

Dr. Blumhofer has left us a glowing appraisal of Mrs.
McPherson's impact on North America. By mid-year 1920,
Sister was becoming a sensation, tapping into deep cultural
yearnings, displaying unusual sensitivity to the popular mood.

In June of 1920, the Lethbridge, Alberta *Daily Herald*
told its readers that the results of Sister's meetings had been
*"so tremendous that anything like a comprehensive record is
impossible to ascertain."* It was the same in Dayton, Ohio;
Alton, Illinois; and Piedmount, West Virginia—everywhere
the response far exceeded expectations.[9]

The Great Montreal Revival

Montreal, Quebec, is considered the largest French-lan-
guage city outside of France. It was here that Aimee Semple
McPherson was invited to conduct three weeks of evangelistic
meetings in Pastor C. E. Baker's largely English-speaking
Pentecostal congregation. What a challenge! They had rented
the ornate and spacious old St. Andrew's Presbyterian Church
on Beaver Hall Hill.

Pastor Baker had been a successful Ottawa businessman.
Only a few years previous to this, his wife had been miraculously
healed of a terminal illness, following which both Mr. and Mrs.
Baker received the baptism in the Holy Spirit and were called to

the ministry. In 1916, after ministering in Ottawa and area, they moved to Montreal to launch a Pentecostal church.

Large Numbers Assemble

In the fall of 1920, Aimee arrived in Montreal, for the three weeks as scheduled. Crowds packed the old church, but the first night it appeared they were off to an inauspicious start. Bats, disturbed by the exceptionally large crowd, swooped out over the congregation. Women began to scream until Mrs. McPherson stood forth in faith and rebuked the scary creatures. They disappeared and were not seen for the rest of the campaign.[10]

Packed Altars

Pastor Baker reported, "*The evening meeting revealed an altar filled with sinners seeking salvation with a prayer room below filled with hungry children of God seeking the baptism of the Holy Spirit. This was just a foretaste of what was to come, as multitudes crowded the building.*"

When prayer was offered for the sick, Pastor Baker wrote, "*What a sight, the lame, halt and blind, seeking deliverance...we will never forget, those who had been bound for so long were now being set free through faith in Jesus' name.*"

Traffic Jams

Mary Naherne, a close friend of the Bakers, reported that the sick were brought on stretchers from the hospitals. Great healings were performed by God's power and broken bodies were healed as Evangelist Aimee Semple McPherson prayed. People went directly from work to church to secure a seat. Traffic was blocked every night in that area.

Problem of Crowd Control

Soon the building, which seated 2,000, was too small and many stood, eager to witness the works of God. Newspaper reporters, amazed at what they saw and heard, were so lost in what they witnessed that they almost forgot their task. The crowds were so intense that policemen were at times unable to cope with them as they pressed to gain entrance.

The response to the altar call was so great that Mrs. McPherson put her hands to her face and exclaimed, "*What shall we do with them? Where shall we put them? Already every available space around the altar and six rows from the front are filled.*"

Strong men came weeping and calling on God to save them from their sins. Men and women, rich and poor, young and old, crowded the altar praying to God for salvation.

In Montreal, Quebec, Pastor C. E. Baker booked the large Old St. Andrew's Presbyterian Church for the meetings.

Holy Spirit Transcends Language Barrier

These meetings touched the francophone community as well. Pastor and Mrs. Dutaud, Baptist pastors, attended the services. Mrs. Dutaud was healed and baptized in the Spirit. This experience was so close to home that it removed all doubt from Pastor Dutaud's mind. He, too, was baptized in the Spirit and became an active Pentecostal worker in Quebec.

Something very remarkable happened in Quebec. Many francophones, although unable to understand the preaching in English, were saved, healed and filled with the Spirit. Mrs. Dutaud reported that her father, Mr. Gregoire, had a crippled arm that had been useless for years. As Mrs. McPherson preached he watched her, not knowing a word that she was saying because he did not understand English, and thought to himself, "*That woman has the face of an angel, not that of a woman.*" At that instant the healing power of God went through him and his crippled arm was made perfectly whole. The impact of these glorious meetings cannot be measured. We will never know how many lives were touched for God and eternity.

15. To God Alone Be Glory!
Soli Deo Gloria

"I Will Lay My Hand on Yours"

One stop was in Baltimore, Maryland.[11] Because news reached reporters of healings God had performed in Aimee's meetings elsewhere, a newspaper headlined her as the "Miracle Woman." The theater was packed with sick people as a result of such publicity. She peeked out at the stretchers and wheelchairs that filled the front, then ran down to the dressing room. She dropped on her knees and said, "*Now, Lord, see what You've done. People up there with broken backs and in casts and wheelchairs. Oh, Lord, I can't heal them.*"

The Lord spoke to her heart. Here was an emergency. The Lord said, "*If those sick are healed and saved, who's going to save and heal them?*"

"*You are, Lord. I can't save or heal one of them,*" she replied.

"*Why are you so nervous? Just go up there and open the Bible,*" the Lord directed. "*You know the Scriptures on healing and salvation. You tell the people what I am going to do, and when you lay your hands on them, I will lay My hand on yours. And all the time you're standing there, I will be standing right back of you. And when you speak the word, I will send the power of the Holy Ghost.*"

You Are Simply the Mouthpiece

"*You are the key on the typewriter. You are only a mouth through which the Holy Ghost can speak. Will you go now?*"

"*Yes, Lord, it is wonderful. I will speak and if they are not healed, it is your business.*"

When the time came, she preached and then prayed for the sick. The Lord told her, "*Now I lay My hand over yours. I AM the Lord that healeth.*" To her surprise, and to her shame, there were more healings that day than she had witnessed in any other place. People with broken backs, Catholics and Protestants, just ran all around the theater. After it was over, the Lord seemed to say to her, "*Remember, if at any time you allow people to call you the 'Miracle Woman' and to say that you healed them, you will have no power. Whatever the results you are to say, 'The glory belongs to the Lord.'*"

16. Showers of Blessings—1921

The year of 1921 saw some of Sister Aimee's greatest meetings ever. The January meetings in San Diego, 140 miles south of Los Angeles, led the way. Many newspaper reports were favorable. After the devastation of World War I, along came Mrs. McPherson offering good news for the present and hope for the future.

Into the "Ring" for Jesus

In Mount Forest Aimee had taken a bold step to gain public attention. Now in San Diego she took advantage of another unusual opportunity to attract the crowd. She had booked the city's Dreamland Arena for a Thursday night. Then she discovered that it was booked for a boxing match on Wednesday, the night before. Those were the very people Aimee wanted at her meetings, so she went to Mr. Keran, the manager, and asked him to introduce her to the boxing crowd between rounds, which he did.

Climbing Through the Ropes

On Wednesday night she made her way through the heavy cigar smoke, climbed through the ropes and spoke to the startled people. She told them about her meetings and challenged them to bring the worst sinner in San Diego next night. It was a bold move, but it won the crowd and made for a good opening on Thursday night when she promised to get into the ring for Jesus. Then she led them in singing,

Give me that old-time religion
It was good for Paul and Silas
It is good for San Diego and
It's good enough for me.

The response was phenomenal. They needed more room and were granted the use of Balboa Park and its 4,000 seat Organ Pavilion for two days. There was prayer for the sick, a huge combined choir and the Salvation Army band in the midst of a sea of humanity.

As Sister stood to speak the congregation burst into song with:

All hail the power of Jesus' name!
Let angels prostrate fall;
Bring forth the royal diadem,
And crown Him Lord of all!

Large Crowds

The San Diego meetings were typical of others that year. The vast size of the crowds made headlines everywhere. The gospel of Jesus Christ, the Good News, became the subject of conversation and multitudes turned to Christ.

A Church in Los Angeles

Soon after Mrs. McPherson settled in Los Angeles, she felt that God was leading her to build a house of worship there, although she did not rush the matter unduly. It was in the January 1921 *The Bridal Call* that Sister first announced intentions to build a church in the city. In September 1921, papers were drawn up which incorporated her work, as indicated in the following statement:

The first formal evidence of the direction she was moving in appeared in legal papers incorporating her work in California. In Los Angeles on September 26, 1921, Aimee, Minnie Kennedy, and Claude Stutsman, a San Jose businessman, and supporter, signed the Articles of Incorporation of Echo Park Evangelistic Association.[12]

Funds for Building

In the course of Aimee's travels leading up to the construction of Angelus Temple, meetings were held in various facilities that seated from 3,000 to 16,000 people. The goal was to preach Jesus and to add souls to the kingdom. As she moved across America, people attending the services enthusiastically gave funds to help with the planned project of establishing a large home church in Los Angeles. The church would serve as a major center of operation for the different ministries that would be initiated. When the opening day arrived they were able to move into a commodious building that was completely free of debt.

The Ideal Property

Prior to incorporating, Sister had spotted a certain area of the city and a specific property which she felt God wanted her to have. This is how she told it:

I was definitely led to a beautiful property with a circular frontage, facing the entrance of peaceful Echo Park. Surely no other piece of land or other location could have been so ideally located—near the center of the city—adjacent to the principal car lines, yet so restfully quiet and apart. The placid lake, the shady trees, the fountain, also the picnic tables, stoves, rest rooms, make the park an ideal place for our congregation to spend the hours between the

services in meditation and prayer, as well as providing
every possible comfort and convenience for the many sick
and afflicted who come for blessing and the healing touch
of the Great Physician.

Real estate agents declared that it was not for sale.
We knew immediately that God had been preserving it
for us. Sure enough, a "For Sale" sign was set up within
a few days by the rich owner who had suddenly decided
she was "land poor."[13]

San Diego Meetings Extended

Such was the continued interest and success in the San
Diego meetings that they were extended twice. The first
plan was for two weeks of meetings; then it was extended
to five weeks. Even after five weeks it seemed they were
only beginning.

First Prolonged Opposition

Mrs. McPherson's meetings reached such magnitude
that they drew both wide attention and some definite opposition. That might have been anticipated, but the source was
disturbing. It came from fellow evangelicals who deliberately
opposed Mrs. McPherson's meetings because they did not
believe divine healing and spiritual gifts were meant for
today. Opposition of this sort usually had little evident effect.
Sometimes it simply drew more attention to the mighty
works of God.

San Jose—1921

The next challenge was in the city of San Jose, California,
where Aimee spent Holy Week ministering in the city's First

Baptist Church. It was the second Baptist church established in California. Over the years it had been instrumental in planting most of the Baptist churches in the San Joaquin Valley.

At this time, its distinguished pastor was William Keeney Towner, who, before coming to California, had pastored several churches in upstate New York. His first California church was Oakland's First Baptist Church, where he had served for eight years, just prior to San Jose. A very energetic man, with a heart for evangelism, he took a bold step in asking Mrs. McPherson to conduct evangelistic services in a Baptist church. Whatever their expectations, both he and Sister Aimee must have been overwhelmed with the results.

San Jose Meetings Defy Description

According to Dr. Edith Blumhofer's report, *"Aimee Semple McPherson stunned San Jose with evangelistic and healing meetings that defied description."* When the first segment of Aimee's meetings in San Jose closed on Easter Sunday, March 27, 1921, the San Jose ministerial followed up with an invitation for her to return for a mammoth, city-wide series of meetings in August and September of 1921. The San Jose meetings of that year certainly were some of the greatest in all of the preacher's outstanding career.

St. Louis—1921

Sister had promised to hold three weeks of meetings in St. Louis even though the sponsoring Assemblies of God church consisted of only sixty-seven members. The invitation was a sign of faith by the church and commitment by the evangelist, who could easily be elsewhere ministering to larger congregations. Time would soon justify the actions of both parties. The small church had rented the large Masonic

Temple, seating 3,000, but they had done little advertising. Perhaps they had spent all available funds on the rent. As it was, local reporters were on hand for the first meeting and reported dramatic testimonies. They witnessed God in action, healing people before their very eyes, miracles that could not be denied.

Within several days, the attendance had grown to such numbers that they needed the police to untangle the traffic and control the crowds. People waited for hours to gain entrance and flowed in like a flood of water as soon as the doors opened. Sister kept close account of converts, noting their church preference. Designated people from those churches followed up by visiting those on their lists. Concluding services were held in the Coliseum, the largest auditorium in the city, on Sunday, May 15. A joint baptismal service took place on the banks of the Mississippi River the next day, as local pastors participated.

17. Revive Us Again—1921 Continued

Three of the cities visited during this year, Denver, Dallas and Rochester, were no strangers to old-time, sawdust trail revivals.

Front Page News

In spite of being a very brief visit to Dallas, a conservative estimate placed the overall attendance at well over 100,000 in total.

The Denver series was sponsored by Arthur C. Peck, a well-known Colorado Methodist minister whose reputation added credence to the meetings. The Denver press wrote up the meetings with an eight-column headline: "*That Woman Is Amazing,*" the *Denver Post* reported.

Miracles of Healing

Although Mrs. McPherson placed the salvation of souls before healing, it must be admitted that genuine, miraculous healings drew people to Christ. This may be the greatest purpose of healing both today and in Bible times. John's Gospel, 20:31, states regarding signs, "*but these are written that you may believe that Jesus is the Christ, the Son of God, and that believing you may have life in His name.*" Jesus mentioned that the healing of a blind man (John 9:3) and the raising of Lazarus from the dead (John 11:15,40) were purposely brought about for the glory of God. One outstanding healing can do more to draw people to God than pages of advertising can.

Not Unto Us, But Unto Your Name Give Glory
(Psalm 115:1)

Aimee Semple McPherson was quick to turn the spotlight off herself and unto God. She made this statement in Denver:

My healings? I do nothing. If the eyes of the people are set on me, nothing will happen. I pray and believe with others, who pray and believe, and the power of Christ works the cure.[14]

Farewell to Denver

Mrs. McPherson left Denver on July 12, 1921. Her automobile, filled with roses, led a line of other cars with well-wishers proceeding from the hotel to Union Station. She then returned to her Los Angeles home for two weeks of rest before engaging in the great San Jose campaign. Plans had already begun for a return to Denver in June of 1922.

San Jose's Second Series—1921

The San Jose ministerial association lent its support to the detailed planning. Aimee and Minnie arrived the day before the opening service to view the huge meeting tent, along with fifty smaller tents for prayer, sleeping, cooking, eating and children's activities. Five hundred additional sites were available for those who brought their own tents.

A Good Start

The first meeting, estimated at 5,000, was on Sunday afternoon, August 8, 1921. William Keeney Towner, pastor of First Baptist Church, took the leading part, backed by a two-hundred-voice volunteer choir, pianos and orchestra. Sister Aimee preached a challenging opening message.

City's Largest Crowd Ever

The numbers grew day by day, as people gathered from out-of-state and Canada. Records indicated that converts were increasing by the hundreds. On Wednesday, August 18, the largest number of people ever gathered in San Jose filled the tent and grounds. Streetcars and automobiles were lined up for blocks. Special services were provided for specific groups, such as the aged and children, so that no one would be left out. By the halfway mark the meetings defied description.

Dr. Charles S. Price Attends

One hundred miles north in Lodi, California, members of the fashionable First Congregational Church were being profoundly changed by these meetings.[15] One day a church member came running across the lawn of the parsonage to greet Pastor Charles Price. Gripping the pastor's hand he exclaimed, *"Brother Price—Hallelujah!—Hallelujah!— Praise the Lord!"*

Dr. Price looked at him with amazement. Expressions like that were not common in his dignified church. The pastor threw back his head to laugh. *"Where have you been?"* he asked.

Clasping the pastor's hand, the member exclaimed, *"Hallelujah—I have been to San Jose and I have been saved— saved—through the blood. I am so happy that I could just float away."* The more his pastor ridiculed him, the more animated he became. Dr. Price, a liberal, modernistic preacher, tried to pass it off as mob psychology, but at the same time an antagonism crept into his heart.

A. B. Forrester

One day A. B. Forrester, another very devout member of the Lodi church, came to Dr. Price and shared his view of the San Jose meetings. Finally, the pastor agreed to attend a service, but first, he inserted an ad in the paper listing his subject for the next Sunday, "Divine Healing Bubble Explodes."

The Skeptic's Search

Dr. Price's automobile rolled south down the highway to San Jose. He read the large sign, "Aimee Semple McPherson, auspices William Keeney Towner." That was a shock to Price. He knew Towner from Oakland days, a splendid, noble, kind man, but not the type, he thought, to be involved in a meeting like this. Price arrived late in the afternoon and was surprised to find such a large tent packed and a great crowd of people standing outside. The afternoon service was just over. The vastness of the crowd amazed him. He elbowed his way into the tent and spotted Dr. Towner coming down the aisle. Towner's face broke into a wreath of smiles. He grabbed Price's hand, "*Charlie Price,*" he said, "*well, hallelujah!— Glory to Jesus!—Praise the Lord!*" When Price drew Towner aside and questioned him, he responded, "*Charlie, this is real. This little woman is right. This is the real gospel. I have been baptized with the Holy Ghost. It is genuine, I tell you. It is what you need.*" After an exchange of a few words Towner shouted, "*Thank God for the baptism,*" shook Price's hand and left, promising to see him later.[16]

Dramatic Change of Heart

What happened in the next few days is a thrilling story. Charles Price ended up at the altar, surrendering all to Jesus

Christ. It was an obvious transformation. Back at his home church in Lodi, he prepared to preach to his people, expecting to be dismissed from his pulpit once his message was delivered. At the conclusion of the service he gave an altar call and to his amazement over eighty people came forward to accept Christ. That was only the beginning of more glorious days ahead.

Spirit Baptism and Miraculous Ministry

Dr. Price received a glorious baptism in the Holy Spirit, such as Jesus promised in Acts, chapter 1. He had gone back to San Jose to tarry in prayer for the baptism in the Holy Spirit. Other seekers, like himself, filled First Baptist Church and the Sunday school rooms. Price, an Oxford graduate and gifted orator, came dressed in his long-tailed Prince Albert coat. He took a piano stool and knelt behind the piano to pray. Some time later Dr. Towner came along with a deacon to move the piano and discovered Dr. Price.

"*What are you doing here?*" he said.

"*I am praying.*"

"*Why don't you get out in the middle of the room?*" Towner asked. He took hold of Price's coat with one hand and the back of his head with the other and said, "*There's too much of this and too much of that.*"

"*I know what you mean,*" Price said.

To make a long story short, Dr. Price began to pray in earnest. Soon he received a wonderful baptism in the Spirit and a call to mass evangelism. He dedicated his natural gifts to God and before long he too was preaching to thousands.

This Saul of Tarsus experience of Dr. Charles Price was a high point in the San Jose meetings. Thousands had been turning to Christ under Mrs. McPherson's ministry; now thousands more were to be brought to the Lord under Dr. Price's ministry.

Conclusion of San Jose Meetings

By the time the McPherson campaign closed, there were over 7,000 professed conversions and around 4,000 had received prayer for healing. Bible days had come again. Memories of those great San Jose meetings are precious.

Canton, Ohio, and Rochester, New York—1921

That fall, Sister traveled east for meetings booked in Canton and Rochester. Seven leading pastors met in Canton's Methodist church and agreed not to cooperate in the meetings. But it was the city's best-known pastor, P. H. Welshimer, who actively opposed. For nineteen years he had been pastor of First Christian Church, the largest church in Canton as well as in his own denomination—no small opponent! Sister, however, refused to be baited but stuck to her regular gospel messages. Crowds streamed into the auditorium. Many came to Christ and prayer was offered for the sick. Some of the ministers changed their minds before a week was over. Dr. Day, the Methodist minister, gave his approval and others followed. Only P. H. Welshimer dared to openly defy Aimee's popularity and doctrine. On the second Sunday he referred to the meetings in a sermon titled "Strange Doctrine," charging that the healings were not divine but were brought about by hypnotism. Then Welshimer decided to hold his own revival services and drew a congregation that filled just over half of his auditorium. His people for the most part stayed with him, but otherwise the McPherson meetings were not affected. Canton's papers gave Sister front page coverage. Welshimer's opposition seemed to enhance rather than diminish Aimee's popularity.

James Kennedy's Death

Sister's father, James Kennedy, had planned to be in Canton for her last Sunday, but, before that, word came that he had passed away in Ingersoll. After the Sunday meeting Aimee took the night train to Ingersoll to attend his funeral.

Numbers of times, James had taken long trips to be in Aimee's meetings. The old gentleman's heart must have swelled with pride and thankfulness as he saw how God was using his daughter. Now he was gone.

Rochester Meetings

Sister Aimee closed the very busy and glorious year of 1921 with three weeks of meetings in Rochester, New York, during the month of November. The city's largest auditoriums were packed as crowds came to hear her.

Students of Christian history in America will be aware that about a century before Aimee's meetings, the city of Rochester was visited with a great revival under Charles G. Finney. But each new generation needs to accept Christ. Without conversions to Christ, the church is only one generation from extinction.

It was David du Plessis who is credited with coining the expression "God has no grandchildren." What he was saying was that to become a Christian each individual person must accept Christ. Your parents cannot do it for you. May God send us more messengers like Finney, Moody, Aimee McPherson and Billy Graham to jar us out of complacency. One generation without conversions to Christ would leave a world without Christians.

Many of Aimee's gypsy followers came from the east and the west to Rochester to attend her meetings.

18. Another Fruitful Year—1922

Early in 1922, Sister was beginning to use the term "Foursquare" to indicate the forming of her doctrinal statement of Christ, the Savior, Healer, Baptizer and Coming King. In essence that was the meaning behind the title "International Church of the Foursquare Gospel," the umbrella organization that included Angelus Temple and others seeking affiliation.

Fresno—1922

Sister's 1922 meetings began in January in the Fresno, California, City Auditorium. It was there that nine-year-old Uldine Utely came to Christ. Within a year she had become a popular child evangelist, preaching to both adults and children. Although this practice did not become common, the first half of the twentieth century saw several child evangelists. Two things helped to give them acceptability—the novelty of a child ministering and their childlike, guileless faith.

San Francisco—1922

Aimee's first venture on radio came in April of 1922. While engaged in three weeks of meetings in San Francisco, Aimee crossed the Bay to Oakland. The Rockridge radio station had offered her radio time on a Sunday morning. Aimee quickly adopted the new medium of implementing the Great Commission. It was a first of many radio broadcasts for her. Soon she would establish her own radio station, KFSG, with radio towers atop the giant temple dome.

It was quite intimidating to face a broadcast microphone for the first time, but in Aimee's case, the good response made her know that the messages were reaching real people out there. In the years prior to the debut of television, North Americans fell in love with radio. It was popular and had tremendous coverage. Evangelicals used the radio waves to proclaim the Good News day and night "across the nation and around the world," as the Assemblies of God Revivaltime motto declared. Radio reached many who might not otherwise have ever heard the Good News. Strong shortwave stations were also established that touched the four corners of the globe.

Wichita—1922

Most of the month of May was spent in Wichita, Kansas. Both positive and negative elements were present, but, as we shall see, the positive outweighed the negative. Members of the ministerial association, like a few others, did not choose to endorse Sister's meetings. One minister warned his people not to attend. He called Aimee a modern Jezebel, an odd designation for one who was proclaiming Christ. It aroused the curiosity of several of his people, who decided to visit the meetings. Harold Jeffries and his wife attended, were converted, and moved to Los Angeles, where they stayed loyal to Aimee for the rest of her life. Disapproval of key local ministers had little effect. Many pastors were won over to Sister's side.

The other negative element ended up bringing glory to God as well. That was the inclement weather. It rained and rained. When a sudden thunderstorm threatened to spoil a service, Aimee rose to her feet, went to the podium and began to pray. This is how she prayed,

Oh Lord stay this rain and this storm...Lord, don't you see these people have come these many miles, and don't

you see, we have come these many miles to preach this word to them. We don't mind going home in the rain, dear Lord, but if it is Thy will, stay it, and if the land hath need of it, let it fall after the message has been delivered to these hungry souls.

The rain stopped instantly, the people marveled and the message was preached. God had answered prayer before their very eyes. It was another vindication of Mrs. McPherson's ministry, and so God blessed the Wichita meetings.

Denver—1922—Kidnapped By the Klan

Following the Wichita meetings, Aimee made a return trip to Denver. Something very unusual took place on that visit. Near the close of an evening meeting Aimee was busy helping at the altar when word came to her that she was wanted to pray for someone in a car outside. With woman reporter Frances Wayne, Aimee made her way outside and they were guided to a waiting car. Two white-robed and hooded men sat on the jump seats with two more in the front. The door slammed shut and the car sped off. One of the masked men assured them that they were safe.

The car stopped and the two women were blindfolded and led into a building crowded with Klansmen. A Klansman stated that they respected her work in Denver and surrounded her with goodwill.

When Aimee was invited to speak she challenged the men to lead lives that would stand the full light of day and stand for righteousness. Their meeting closed and the women were escorted back safely.

No more was heard from the Klan until the final night in Denver. Two hooded figures showed up at Sister's hotel room door and handed her a bag of money that they had collected as a gift for her children. Sister and the Klan were miles apart on racism and other issues. They knew it too but apparently wanted to indicate that they had no intention of interfering with her or her work.

Ministering in Oakland—1922

In July, Sister held special meetings in Oakland. Enthusiastic crowds gave Aimee and Minnie a rousing welcome upon their arrival at the train station. The city witnessed remarkable meetings from the beginning. Oakland had a number of groups that promoted new thought, divine science and spiritualist meetings, whose philosophies were diametrically opposed to Aimee's. Yet she stood firm. The total attendance for all services reached some 200,000.

The meetings opened with a Saturday night rally followed by a Sunday afternoon, July 17, capacity crowd of 7,000. The sermon title was "The Four Square Gospel." Nineteen states and Canada were represented in the audience. Over 600 responded to the altar call for salvation.

Children's Rally

Aimee conducted a children's rally the day before her Oakland meetings closed. The stage was heaped with toys and candy that had been donated. These were distributed to the children along with an autographed Bible for every child. There was multicultural participation as the children sang and recited their parts.

Seniors gathered for their own meeting in the afternoon. Aimee wanted every group to have something for their age.

The Australian Tour—1922

This long-awaited trip began five days after the Oakland meetings closed. More than a thousand gathered at dockside for Aimee and Minnie's send-off on the S.S. Manganaui as they sang, "God be with you till we meet again."

The month-long voyage could have been a time for leisure, but Sister found plenty of work to do on *The Bridal Call* and many details in preparation for the opening of the Temple, planned to take place shortly after their return in December.

Melbourne

Mrs. McPherson began her Australian meetings in Melbourne. Upon discovering that the party who had originally invited her held differing doctrinal views, particularly on the deity of Christ, Aimee made the decision to launch out on her own. She had no trouble winning the support of the news media. The following is a sample of a press statement:

Mrs. McPherson possesses a magnificent platform appearance...Her personality is magnetic, with a joyous vitality that is mental as well as physical; and her smile is a wholesome, hearty beam that calls "Cheerio" to the world in general.[17]

Adelaide

Reports from Melbourne preceded her, and the Adelaide reception was the same. The response of the people was very favorable. They appreciated the way that Aimee shared the message of the love of Jesus Christ. They also accepted her healing ministry and the fact that she was a woman preacher.

Sydney

After a series of meetings in Sydney, Aimee and Minnie
sailed home to America.

19. Angelus Temple:
Grand Opening—1923

While Aimee was on her Australian tour, activity did not cease back in Los Angeles. If anything, the pace picked up in anticipation of the opening of Angelus Temple on January 1, 1923. That morning, at the temple site, workers and volunteers rushed to make sure all was in readiness for the afternoon opening at 2:30 p.m. Brook Hawkins, the builder-architect, was directing where last pieces of carpet should be laid and the placing of potted trees, palms and flowers. He draped giant American and Canadian flags on the two long ramps that descended from the left and right sides of the balconies to the platform. The Steinway concert grand piano and a golden harp were each set in place. Outside, carpenters were erecting a temporary platform facing Echo Park. Everything was to be ready for the opening of the doors at 2:30 p.m.

The Temple Float

Before dawn, other temple volunteers had gathered to decorate a float to be entered on that day in the Pasadena Tournament of Roses parade. Aimee had obtained the largest truck she could find. Professionals directed workers as they constructed a replica of Angelus Temple on the flat bed and decorated it with thousands of pink roses and white carnations.

A musician sat inside the replica, playing familiar hymns and gospel melodies on a pump organ while fifteen girls sang as they rode along among the flowers. A reverent hush came over the spectators as the float passed by. Signs on the float and flyers announced the opening of Angelus Temple that afternoon.

First Prize

The float won first prize in its division. It provided excellent publicity for the temple. Who knows how many viewers were influenced? A Canadian family by the name of Griffin was in Los Angeles at the time. They saw the float, went to the Temple, accepted Christ as Savior, received the baptism in the Holy Spirit and later returned to Canada. They were one of the first founding families of the Pentecostal church in Hamilton, Ontario. George B. Griffin, a son, became a well-known pastor. At least three generations of the Griffin family have entered the Pentecostal ministry. Who knows how many more were similarly influenced by the float that first year?

Angelus Temple's Beauty

One would have to see the structure of the Temple to appreciate its size and beauty. Aimee described it in these words:

At last it was done. The largest fireproof, Class A, church in America. It is constructed of concrete and steel with multi-colored rays piercing great thirty-foot stained glass windows which I designed during the journey from San Francisco to Sydney, Australia. Each window depicts a phase in the life of our dear Savior. Beautiful Angelus Temple! How I love it.[18]

The gleaming white building sits on an oval shaped lot. Its many front doors open into the foyer. A full width, semicircular auditorium rising up to the spacious dome above seats 5,300.

The Great Event

By noon on opening day thousands crowded the street, sidewalk and park about the church. Police had to divert traffic to make room for more. It was a time of joyous expectancy as the waiting crowd took up one hymn after another.

At 2:15 p.m. on the dot, Sister McPherson stepped onto the outside platform to begin the formal opening. Dr. Gale of Oakland Baptist Church offered the dedicatory prayer. Sister then led the over 5,000 assembled in singing "All Hail the Power of Jesus' Name." Then she turned in her Bible to 1 Kings 8 and read the account of Solomon dedicating the first temple in Jerusalem. She knelt as she read Solomon's prayer, then stepped down to the street and took trowel and mortar to lay the cornerstone. After unveiling two tablets commemorating the occasion, she prayed another prayer of dedication. The crowd burst into song. Aimee stepped aside, the doors swung open and the multitude flowed in, filling the 5,300-seat auditorium in a matter of minutes.

First Service

The first service inside Angelus Temple opened with a stirring rendition of "Holy, Holy, Holy," led by the white-robed Temple choir. Then, surrounded by minister friends from different denominations, Sister took Brook Hawkins's arm and made her first entrance down the right-hand ramp. For the next few hours, music filled the Temple, interspersed with prayer and short addresses by visiting clergy. Immediately after a soloist sang Fanny Crosby's "Open the Gates of the Temple," Sister moved to the pulpit and, with tears in her eyes, asked the congregation to join her in singing the doxology. Then she read from the Old Testament book of Ezra about the joy the Israelites expressed when they returned from captivity to rebuild the temple in Jerusalem. She preached on worship, incorporating the story of her life in an overview of Old Testament altars. Although in one sense Salford, Ontario, was now remote, Sister brought it to center stage at this supreme moment in her life. She stood amid the adulation of adoring thousands of Americans as a Canadian farm girl who had made good. The huge auditorium was charged with emotion as she led in the singing of the first of her "Foursquare Gospel battle songs":

> *Preach the Foursquare Gospel, the Foursquare Gospel,*
> *Clear let the Foursquare message ring:*
> *Jesus, only Savior, Baptizer and Healer,*
> *Jesus the Coming King.*

Sister could not pass up the opportunity for an altar call. Hundreds pressed forward, among them scores of the gypsies who sat in a reserved section of the main floor. They laid floral tributes on the stage. Grateful gypsies had contributed generously to the Temple, giving its "Calvary" stained glass window, its velour stage curtains and the hand-carved wooden letters of Hebrews 13:8, "Jesus Christ the same yesterday, today, and forever," across the proscenium.

For Sister, January 1, 1923, stood out as *"the greatest— the crowning day of fifteen years of ministry—the day when the seemingly impossible was realized, the glorious dream had become an actual reality."*[19]

The Blessing Continues

The following is a quote from *The Personal Testimony of Aimee Semple McPherson*, page 60, completed and published in 1928; revised, expanded and edited by Dr. Leitia Mae Steward. Consultants: Dr. Rolph K. McPherson and Dr. Raymond Cox.

From the moment the Temple was opened, on January 1, 1923, the crowds came. In spite of its 5,300 seats, the great auditorium was taxed to capacity nightly. Revival spirit ran high, the altars were filled and 12,000 were converted the first year. Miracles of healing, so real and so evident even to the unbeliever, brought a thoughtful world to our doors and to our altars.

Hundreds were filled with the Holy Spirit and students came from far and near to study at our Bible School. Thousands were prayed for by our workers in the Prayer Tower, who ministered 24-hours-a-day, and were also ministered to through our commissary which provided the food and clothing.

During the first five years more than 1,200 have joined the Temple annually, more than 10,000 each year have wept their way to the altar and more than 3,000 have been baptized in water. A special siding was built by the electric railroad company near the church and special trains, many cars long, were run to every service. During the big meetings on week nights and three times on Sunday, that siding is jammed with cars waiting to take the multitudes.[20]

20. New Horizons

After the Temple Opening

Building the Temple was the high point in fifteen years of ministry, but by no means did it imply that a stationary plateau had been established. It was rather a platform upon which to build and go forward with new ventures for God.

A Great Home Base

The copious facilities of Angelus Temple furnished new and greater possibilities. Sister could now live at home and minister right at hand. Without leaving the city she had a pulpit, commodious auditorium, built-in radio station (1924) and office facilities, all within steps of her residence. They were available twenty-four hours a day, seven days a week. It was a great convenience, although her lack of privacy should be weighed against that.

ANGELUS TEMPLE
CHURCH OF THE
FOUR SQUARE GOSPEL

AIMEE SEMPLE McPHERSON
- FOUNDER -

Dramatization

Aimee Semple McPherson was a professional when it came to employing drama to portray her messages. It was a gift she possessed since childhood and now she could use it to the full. To augment her own ability she had at hand one of the finest auditoriums with excellent acoustics.

Hollywood with its gifted artists and professional props was close at hand. It is said that Charlie Chaplin gave Aimee advice on a better stage arrangement for her illustrated sermons. When Aimee was ministering at home in the Temple, dramatic productions were so much more easily prepared and produced.

People loved her productions and crowded in to see them. These illustrated sermons drew a greater number of the public to being exposed to the truth of the gospel of Jesus Christ, "the greatest story ever told." In turn it brought more converts to Christ. If Sister was criticized for employing theatrical methods, she probably felt that the results had justified the means. Many of her associates in smaller congregations followed Aimee's lead and produced illustrated messages, albeit with a lesser degree of professionalism.

A Bible College

The concept of a training institute for pastors, missionaries and evangelists had been in Aimee's mind right from the beginning. It was a logical step, in that it would serve those who flocked to the Temple and desired to give their lives in full-time service for God. If the Foursquare Church was going to spread out and establish new congregations they needed an institution to train new workers.

The school opened on February 1, a month after the Temple. It was located in the administration building next door. Fifty students registered for the opening day, but the attendance continued to grow until the space was inadequate.

A Separate Building

Plans were made to erect a five-and-a-half-story building that would care for not only the Bible school but for 3,000 Sunday school children. The cornerstones were laid on April 26, 1925, with the official opening and dedication January 3, 1926. It was a beautiful building of steel and concrete. One auditorium seated 1,500 (which could be used for overflow congregations). There were almost 1,000 students constantly registered. It became officially known as L.I.F.E. Bible College, the full title being "Lighthouse of International Foursquare Evangelism." In the years since its founding, thousands of students have been trained, ordained and sent forth to serve.

Well-known Faculty Members

Perhaps the best-known instructor was Frank Thompson, who was responsible for creating the extensive notes for *The Thompson Chain Reference Bible*, which has been popular worldwide for many years. Another noted faculty member was Dr. Lilian B. Yeomans, a medical doctor who had been miraculously delivered from drug addiction. She ministered from a background of personal experience and now gave herself to full-time ministry. Both Thompson and Yeomans had moved to California in late life and were readily available to contribute to L.I.F.E. Bible College.

A Pioneer in Radio

In the early 1920s, radio came into its own, a powerful force of communication. Like many lesser-known Pentecostal pastors, Aimee was always ready to utilize each new phase of the media to spread the gospel. Operators of Los Angeles radio stations had told her that she could build her own station at the Temple for $25,000. By 1924, there were 200,000 receiving sets within a hundred-mile radius of the city, and they were increasing.

Aimee's people readily responded to the opportunity of entering this new door of opportunity. She hired Kenneth G. Ormiston, radio engineer from the Times-Mirror station, and commissioned him to build a modern broadcast studio on the third floor of the Temple. In the light of some events that followed, it should be noted that Ormiston was not a member of the Temple and probably did not share Aimee's view and vision from a Christian perspective, but he was capable of building and operating the facility.

On the Air—"Give the winds a mighty voice!"

The station was ready for operation on February 6, 1924, using the call letters KFSG (Kall Four-Square Gospel). Its towers stood atop the building, rising above the great white dome. Soon airwaves from the Temple carried the Good News in word, music and song. It was a powerful instrument for the propagation of the gospel, potentially capable of reaching every home within radius.

It was an instant success. Every morning that Aimee was home, she broadcast live at 7:00 a.m. Her voice became one of the most familiar in the United States. Some of the finest speakers, musicians and vocalists could be heard over KFSG. One can only imagine how Sister could have employed television in her repertoire.

The KFSG transmitting towers above Angelus Temple illustrated Aimee's burning desire to spread the Good News to all who would hear.

Radio Used to Full Advantage

One morning, Sister received a phone call before dawn. A member who had moved to Santa Barbara called to report a devastating earthquake there. People needed help, and soon. Aimee broke into a radio program and made the announcement that Santa Barbara, one hundred miles north, had experienced a severe earthquake and was in urgent need of emergency supplies. She appealed for donations of food and clothing and called for those who had trucks to fill their tanks with gas and come and load up for the trip north. Before a special edition of the *Los Angeles Times* hit the streets, the first convoy of supplies from the Temple was on its way. By the time the Red Cross convened a meeting, the second convoy from Angelus Temple had already arrived with blankets and food for the homeless.

Benevolence

Before many current agencies were formed, Aimee's Temple band was organized and ready to respond to such emergencies, large or small. It was not just a case of efficiency but also compassion flowing from the love of God. They were flexible and ready to reach out quickly to the homeless and helpless.

A Commissary

Perhaps the modern term *food bank* had not been coined when Aimee set up the Angelus Temple Commissary. She put it under the direction of a well-organized group of women known as the Foursquare City Sisters. This is not to suggest that there were not other benevolent groups, but the Temple was right in there, ministering in Christ's compassion. This continued into and through the Great Depression. A fifteen-foot-tall lighthouse was set up in the church lobby as a collection point. So much were they committed to helping the needy that it taxed the finances of the Temple during the hardest years of the thirties.

Storm Clouds Looming

The honeymoon with the press continued well after the Temple opening. A great work was being done for both the spiritual and social welfare of the city of Los Angeles. But Aimee's popularity did not last forever. For that matter, popularity is fleeting. When winds of adversity start to blow ripples on placid water, it may soon turn into gale force winds whipping up a storm. This analogy was true in Aimee's case. Using hindsight, we can see how little ripples of opposition joined forces and gathered momentum, seeking not only to vilify Aimee but to destroy her.

An Enemy at Work

Jesus told a parable about a man who sowed good seed in his field, but at night, while men slept, his enemy came and sowed tares among the wheat and went his way. When the grain sprouted, the tares appeared also (Matthew 13:24-30).

Aimee had experienced great success, abundant harvests, as it were, with very little opposition. Her enemy, Satan, was well aware of what was going on and was biding his time for the opportune moment to sweep in and deal a devastating blow calculated to destroy her. Life is like that. Jesus warned His disciples that if the world hated Him it would also hate them (John 15:18-19), but He promised to sustain them and not allow them to be tested above what they could endure (See 1 Cor. 10:13).

Annie Johnson Flint wrote:

God hath not promised
Skies always blue,
Flower strewn pathways
All our lives through;
God hath not promised
Sun without rain,
Joy without sorrow,
Peace without pain.

But God hath promised
Strength for the day,
Rest for the labor,
Light for the way,
Grace for the trials,
Help from above,
Unfailing sympathy,
Undying love.

Detractors

There were envious faultfinders out there, and even a few in the church, just ready to pounce upon any opportunity to belittle Aimee. Her ministry put her in a place of prominence and set her up as a target for dissenters. She had not been hesitant to publicly denounce deliberate crimes and corruption, even over the radio station. And criminal elements were not prepared to allow that to continue. Authorities also felt the pressure of exposure. The slightest hint of an opportunity to discredit Sister Aimee in the eyes of the public would be welcome. She was a formidable foe against all that was evil in society, but they did not know just how to bring her down. Make no mistake about it: bring her down they felt they must. Then the opportunity came.

There had been warning signs of the one thing that would strike a devastating blow—kidnapping. She was a prime target, extremely popular with thousands of loyal followers whose loyalty would prompt them to come to her aid should a ransom be demanded. Aimee was well known, yet she moved freely among the public, making it comparatively easy to watch for the ideal situation to snatch her away.

Sister had ignored numerous notes threatening kidnapping or death. She passed them off as the work of cranks. In 1925, reporters claimed to have uncovered a plot to abduct her, but she dismissed it. (See *The Verdict Is In* by Raymond L. Cox, Salem, Oregon, 13.)

On one occasion a man who had been writing hostile notes with threats to blow up the Temple forced his way into Aimee's home, frightening the women and children. Carpenters working nearby intervened and held the man until police arrived. Early in 1925, police uncovered a plot to kidnap Aimee and hold her for ransom (Blumhofer, p. 290). Then, it really did happen!

21. Kidnapped

Mrs. McPherson wrote her account of the kidnapping with many details, which was published in the August 1926 issue of *The Bridal Call*, pages 25-31. The following account draws heavily on Mrs. McPherson's report.

It happened so suddenly on May 18, 1926. Aimee Semple McPherson, pastor of the 5,300 seat Angelus Temple in Los Angeles, had just returned from a short shopping trip downtown at Bullocks Department Store.

Her mother, Minnie Kennedy, noticed how pale and tired Aimee appeared and suggested that she take the afternoon off with an outing at the beach. Aimee agreed. She could rent an umbrella, go for a swim and work on her notes for the meeting that night. Her secretary, Emma Schaeffer, gladly went along. They headed off to Ocean Park Beach. As was her custom, Aimee changed her clothing at Ocean View Hotel. Frank Langan, the manager, had urged her to use their facilities when she came to the beach.

The two women had a snack at a concession before renting and pitching an umbrella tent on the sand. Aimee did some work on her sermon, then went for a dip in the ocean. Returning to the tent, she attempted some modifications on the travelogue she was presenting that evening. It was then that she realized her need to inform her musical director to prepare two new slides, so she sent Emma to call him by phone while she went for another swim.

"All right," Emma agreed. Aimee was a strong swimmer, but Emma begged, "Don't go too far now."

As Mrs. McPherson started into the water she heard

someone call her name. We now turn to her personal account of the matter:

Turning, I saw a man and a woman standing at the edge of the water. Even in my brief hour of recreation the call of duty was never silent for long.

Making my way to the shore, I looked into the faces of the couple solicitously, for both seemed under great nervous stress. The woman was visibly trembling and looked on the verge of tears.

"Oh, my baby!" she said. "My baby! She is dying. The doctor has given her up. Oh, Sister, come and pray for her! Won't you? You will come!"

"We have her right here in the car." This eagerly from the man, who stood twisting his hat in his hands.

"But I can't go now. You will have to wait until I get dressed."

"No! No! I have a coat here."

Suiting the action to the words, a large loose coat like a mackintosh was thrown over my shoulders. I slipped my arms into the loose sleeves, noting with approval that it came well down toward my feet.

The woman ran ahead to the car while the man walked by Aimee's side.

We approached the car from the rear. The door was open. A man sat at the wheel. The woman sat in the far side of the back seat, holding a bundle of blankets or shawls, which I presumed to be the baby, in her arms, gently rocking and crooning. "You had better step in," said the man. "You can reach the baby better."

Only too glad to do this, being barefooted, I stepped on the running board, my weight thrown forward.

Then upon me, utterly unsuspecting, trusting in them, fell this terrible thing. Dear Lord! I have lived it through a thousand times since then. Shall I ever forget it?—the quick strong shove, just beneath my shoulders, that threw me forward on my face and arms so that I fell to the floor of the car.

A smothering, suffocating mass of blankets over me—a hand that held something that felt like sponge on my face—a sticky, sweet odor, a gasp, a struggle, a firm hand at the back of my head, the roar of a motor and it grew dark.

When Aimee regained consciousness, she found herself in a room lying in a white iron bed, desperately nauseated. The same woman was bending over her. The room was strange to her, blue and pink wallpaper, an old dresser, a cot and chair and boarded windows.

"You are the lady with the baby," I said. "Where am I? What has happened?"

Without answering my question definitely, the woman, who later told me I might call her "Rose," called two men from the adjoining room. One was the man who had accompanied her to the beach, and the other, the man who sat behind the wheel of the car. They stood at the foot of my bed. They answered my questions, but the answers seemed to freeze the blood in my veins.

What were they saying? Held for ransom! Why? Nonsense! Surely I was dreaming. One read of such things in the papers. They happened to others, but never could they happen to me! Was I dreaming? A nightmare?

"But it is ridiculous!" I protested. "I must go back! I have to address an audience! My mother will be frantic! My children—the training school—it is

examination time! My papers are all to be corrected. There is the radio—the people, the—the—Why, you must take me back!"

"Oh, you will go back, all right," they said, "when we get what we want."

Dully I lay there and watched until the two men left the room. The woman, who was my constant attendant, who slept in the room with me, who took what I would suppose one would call good care of me, under the circumstances, had left the room also for a moment.

Arising from the bed, I made my way to the window and gave shout after shout. It was but a moment until the three were in the room again and ordered me to stop that. Later I tried it again, but the man they called "Steve" and the woman held me and put a wad of white cloth in my mouth and tied it firmly behind my head. They removed it shortly afterward and told me if I called out again I would be gagged and stay that way.

Looking at the words after they are written, I shake my head and feel that it was all a mistake—that it could not, just could not have happened. It all seems too melodramatic, too far-fetched, too unreasonable and strange; but it did happen, and of all the people in the world, it happened to me whose well-ordered life was filled with incessant duties of ministering to the sinful, the sick, the dying and the needy. Day after day, night after night, this one room was my habitation. I lost all track of day and date. Hour after hour, day after day, I lay on the bed or paced that little room. My thoughts ran in an endless circle, the picture of my prison and my jailers were burned on my mind. I can close my eyes and see it all.

Where had I been taken in that car, while I lay unconscious under the smothering blankets? In what lonely, hidden place was I a prisoner?

There was running water in the house, but how much did that mean? The water might be piped from a well or we might possibly be on the edge of some town. There was neither comfort nor cheer in my prison room, only the merest necessities.

Back at Ocean Park Beach

When Emma Schaeffer returned to the beach after making the phone call she looked in vain for Sister. She was not in the umbrella tent, nor on the beach. She scanned the water, but there was no sign of Aimee. Finally, she called the Temple office to inform them that Sister had gone swimming and was missing. The immediate conclusion by most, and Minnie in particular, was that Aimee had drowned.

A Strange Twist of Irony

As clever as the kidnappers were, and as smoothly as they carried out their operation, they had made a fatal mistake. When a person goes missing at a beach the natural supposition is that they have drowned. No one would be so naive as to pay a ransom in such a scenario. Aimee's followers flocked to the beach and searched for hours. (Years later, one of those searchers was a member of the author's church and related these things to him.) So convinced were Minnie and others of Aimee's drowning that a special memorial service was held in her memory. That put extra pressure on the kidnappers to prove they had Aimee in their custody. They plied Sister with questions about her childhood home, things that only she and Minnie knew, so they could convince Minnie and the Angelus Temple congregation that Aimee was being held for ransom.

Aimee's Refusal to Cooperate

When they said they were holding me for five hundred thousand dollars, I refused to answer the questions, saying I would rather die than cripple the church to such an extent.

"I won't answer your questions—not one of them!" I exclaimed.

"You will if you know what is for your own good. You will answer them and answer them quick," said a gruff voice, and a strong hand fell upon my wrist. A lighted cigar butt was placed to first one finger and then another. There are still, at the moment of writing, scars on my fingers, though some weeks have passed.

Instead of showing fear, somehow I had the presence of mind to keep perfectly steady, though I winced a little. Looking up into their faces, I said, " Go ahead." A little shamefacedly, he desisted.

The Hiding Place

The man they called Steve was absent many days, presumably trying to arrange a ransom deal. One night, after he had been away for several days, Aimee heard the men talking angrily, cursing and swearing. Scraps of conversation drifted into her room. They suggested that if Minnie did not pay up, they would sell Aimee to a man named Felipe in Mexico City. They seemed to be getting desperate.

Changing Location

Most of Sister's captivity was in the same house—day after day, night after night. Then there was a hurried departure. Perhaps they thought they were in danger of being discovered.

One night I was asleep when Rose awakened me and told me to get up and dress. Evidently they had suddenly decided to move. I was blindfolded and taken out and put in the car. The right half of the front seat of the car had been folded forward, A narrow mattress, evidently the one from Rose's cot, had been laid upon the floor, and I was placed upon it, my hands and my feet tied firmly, but quite comfortably.

Then began a long trip. During the journey, I recall but one or two stops and these seemed to be in the country. One was to put in gasoline, which I believe was carried in an extra can. Only once during the trip was I gagged. I remember that at the time there was a rumble, as of some traffic, as though we might be passing through a town. I was helpless, lying there with my hands and feet tied in the bottom of the car. Oh, if they only would have to stop somewhere near human habitation. Even if they gagged me, surely I could make some sort of a disturbance that would attract attention. My feet were tied but I could kick the sides of the car. But they did not stop where such a thing was possible. Once or twice the car slowed down and I thought—"Now perhaps I can do it." But there was no sound of voices outside the car. It might have been in the country.

Rose and the dark man, whose name I never heard, were in the car. The man drove. Rose sat in the back seat. Steve, I think must have gone in the other car with the camp equipment, for there was nothing like that in the car that carried me.

How long that day was! We drove on and on. Sometimes the roads were smooth, sometimes rough. I could not see out. My head was far below the level of the car windows. The day passed and darkness had once more fallen.

Second Hideout

Aimee was taken from the car, blindfolded and hurried into a room in some house or shack. It was a small, dark room with army cots and blankets. There was a pail and a dipper in one corner and a big tin can with jagged edges. It was so hot. Aimee felt weak and discouraged. How long would this last? Would she ever be free again to see her family, home and friends?

A day or so later, Aimee could not remember how long, the men left. She heard the car start and she was left alone with Rose. Aimee remembers Rose coming to her with some flat strips of cotton cloth. "Now dearie," she said, "I must go for provisions. I'll have to tie you for a little while. I'll soon be back."

Please tie my hands in front of me, then," I begged. "My arms and shoulders get so stiff when my hands are behind me."

Rose shook her head. "Lie down on your side," she said. There was nothing for me to do but to obey. She tied my hands behind me. My feet were crossed and tied that way. The cloth was not tied tightly enough to hurt, yet enough to hold me.

Rose went out and I heard a car start. The engine sounded like that of a small car with a light motor. There were no voices outside and I was quite sure the men had not returned.

A Chance to Escape

It was the first time I had been left alone. Possibly I was so weak now, not having felt able to stand for more than a few minutes the last days, that she felt it safe to go for supplies.

At any rate now was my great opportunity for escape, if only I was strong enough. Could I make it? Desperation and hope lent strength to my weakened frame. I prayed with all my soul for power to thrust back the weakness that was upon me, for the mist to clear from my tired mind. "Oh, give me strength—Lord, give me strength!" I prayed. My ankles had been crossed in the tying. It was impossible for me to walk, even in short steps. I rolled from the cot and across the floor. There by the wall stood a square tin can, like an oil can. The top had been cut away in such a manner as to leave a sharp edge.

Lifting myself with difficulty to a sitting posture, I managed to turn my back to the can and press the bands that bound my wrist against the sharp edge. Awkwardly, but persistently, I sawed the bonds against its edge, until at last one strand parted. My wrists became chaffed and bruised, but it was done and in a moment my hands were free.

Loosing my feet and chaffing my ankles, I stood up. I could walk. I reached the window and climbed out, and like the man in the Bible days, "I stood out on the order of my going." I ran straight ahead—ran and ran—and was only stopped by a sharp pain in my side. The mist of fear and haste that had clouded my vision cleared a little, and I took stock of my surroundings. I was in a desert. Rolling country, covered with growths, with which I was not familiar, stretched out for what seemed to be endless miles. By the sun, I would judge it to be about eleven o'clock in the morning.

At any moment the car might return and my absence be noticed. Which way was I headed? That did not matter either. The main thing was to get away, anywhere. On, on I sped. The sun was blazing down hotly, but having on a long white cotton underslip, I was able to turn my dress over my head and arms as protection from the burning rays.

Down through little gullies, up over little knolls, on across level stretches of country, weaving in and out among the desert growth, stumbling sometimes, yet going on and on, ever on until the sun was growing low. No human soul did I see.

Afterwards, it was charged that her shoes showed no sign of wear and tear. It should be noted that she was walking in sand dunes, not hard ground.

I should judge it would be about five-thirty o'clock in the afternoon when, exhausted and thirsty, I determined to head for a certain dark hill which stood out above the rest and which I later learned to be Niggerhead Mountain. Possibly here there would be water or shelter.

When I reached the hill the moon was shining brightly and all the stars were looking down upon the desert. It was a beautiful sight, but I, who loved the heavens, was in no mood for enjoying their glory on this night. Stark terror had taken hold of me. I remembered many stories of people who had died in the desert, hopelessly lost, perishing for food and water.

From an elevation at the foot of the mountain she saw a distant glow of light, indicating a place of habitation, a sign of hope at least. Winding her way down the slope, she came upon a road that showed signs of travel. With fresh courage, she pressed on in spite of sore feet and trembling knees. She felt so thirsty and weary that she thought of spending the night in the desert. She scooped up some sand and put her skirt over it and for a pillow, but she could not rest, so staggered on. How far could it be? Finally she came upon a little building, but there was no sign of life—deserted. The cool of the night was a blessing, but the sounds in the darkness around frightened her and she thought of rattlesnakes and lizards.

She heard dogs barking in the distance. Finally, she came upon a large building. She called out and a man's voice answered her. He told her it was a slaughterhouse. There was a fence between them. It was the border between Mexico and the United States. She was on the Mexican side. He invited her to come through the fence, but his manner was a bit too friendly, so she declined and pressed on.

Finally she came to a nice house with a hedge about it. It looked promising, but the people were reluctant to take a stranger in at that time of the night. She turned away but fell exhausted at their gate. At last the man and woman came to help her. They thought she was dying, but when they saw signs of life, they moved her to the piazza and covered her with blankets. When she roused she called, "Water! Water!" and "Where am I?" They told her she was in Mexico, in the town of Prieta and that Douglas, Arizona, was nearby.

She kept asking them to get the police. Finally, an American taxi driver offered to take her to the Douglas hospital. There she told them that she was Aimee Semple McPherson, but they did not believe it. At first they thought she was a drunk who had crossed the border. Then a man came, looked at her, paced up and down and finally asked,

"Would you mind blowing your breath in my face—just once?"
"Why no," I replied, not realizing what he might mean by such a request.

The Breath Test

They thought I had been drinking and was imagining I was Mrs. McPherson. I did what he asked, and forever settled that idea.

They told me they would telephone to Los Angeles, to the police and to my mother. I could scarcely hold the receiver, scarcely control my voice. "Hello, darling."

And back over those miles of wires came the voice I thought I would never hear again. "Aimee! Oh, thank God! Thank God! Aimee!"

And in that Douglas hospital, I breathed the same prayer of joy: "Thank God! Oh, thank God."

Dr. Edith Blumhofer's account states as follows on page 287:

Later that day, Minnie Kennedy, Roberta Semple, Rolf McPherson, police captain Herman Cline, his son-in-law deputy district attorney Joseph Ryan, and fourteen reporters and newsreel photographers boarded a special Pullman car for the 550-mile ride to Douglas, Arizona. When the train pulled in at the station at eight the next morning, a crowd was on hand to welcome them. A long caravan followed Minnie and the children in one car and the police and reporters in others to the hospital where Sister—propped up on pillows in a hospital bed—awaited them.[21]

Aimee, though not over her ordeal, obliged the media with a full report of all that had happened. What a shock it must have been when she discovered some did not believe her!

A Grand Welcome Home!

At 9:13 p.m. on Friday, June 25, Mrs. McPherson and her family left Douglas, Arizona, for Los Angeles on the Southern Pacific Railroad's Golden State Limited.

Two thousand people gave them an affectionate send-off.

What a contrast with her entry! At every stop along the way that night crowds met the train and clamored to see Sister.

Los Angeles Police prepared for a crowd that some thought might exceed the 25,000 that had shown up to welcome Sister home from Palestine nearly two months before. At 1:30 p.m. Saturday, the crowd was estimated at 4,000 and growing by the minute. As the train neared the station at 2:45 at least 50,000 packed the pavement for blocks. Every bit of rooftop, pavement and fencing was covered for a mile out of the station. The sweet sound of hymns and choruses filled the air. Temple bands and choirs played and sang "Wonderful Savior" as the train rolled into the station. Her automobile, covered with flowers, took an unplanned parade to Angelus Temple.

June 26, 1926. The evangelist had been missing more than a month. Many of the approximately 50,000 who greeted her train in Los Angeles had been earnestly praying for her safe return. It was estimated that Aimee passed 100,000 well-wishers on her way home.

Sister walked down the ramp to the pulpit to give a report of the terrible ordeal. Her people and thousands of the general populace believed in her, despite false charges and rumors that were being circulated. Specific rebuttals are given in the next chapter.

22. Vindicated

There is an old saying, "A lie goes around the world before truth gets its boots on." That seems to apply in Aimee Semple McPherson's case. Even before she left Arizona there were accusations, questions and innuendoes. Detractors were quite vocal in their allegations. But Aimee was consistent and never varied in her account of what happened.

Why the Animosity?

Why would anyone question the story or the motives of this good lady? For one thing, they were not prepared to acknowledge that she was a good and honest person. If we consider the reaction to Christ in His day it gives us some idea for the hostile attitude shown toward Aimee.

When Jesus stood before the Roman Governor, Pontius Pilate, accused by the religious leaders, the Bible says that Pilate knew their motive. *"For he knew that they had handed Him over because of envy"* (Matthew 27:18). There are connotations linked with the word envy, such as jealousy, bitterness, and resentment, yet Jesus was without sin. The only accusations they could bring against Him were false. Pilate declared in Luke 23:4, *"I find no fault in this Man."*

Even Judas, Christ's betrayer, filled with remorse, cried out, *"I have sinned by betraying innocent blood"* (Matthew 27:4).

What Motivated Sister's Opponents?

Mrs. McPherson's enemies were bitter and resentful because she publicly exposed corruption and named names, so they wanted to discredit and silence her. Her standards brought people under conviction for their own sins. This could have had a bearing on the attitude of Los Angeles' District Attorney Asa Keys, who himself was later sentenced to penitentiary on unrelated charges. He pursued her relentlessly in an effort to prove her guilty.

They were looking for any excuse to bring her down. Rather than diligently pursuing kidnappers, they sought to charge Aimee and her mother Minnie with criminal conspiracy. The word *envy* suggests another reason. Some are always envious of those who attain popularity and success.

The Press' Involvement

How much influence did the Los Angeles press have on the case? A long, drawn-out court case of almost ninety consecutive days was treated as sensational news and the news sold papers, which meant revenue. Someone said, "Good Aimee is no news. Bad Aimee is real news." Bad news made "good" headlines from their perspective.

When there was a public outcry about the cost to the county, Keyes announced that the newspapers had underwritten most of the expense of the investigation. The district attorney could not prove Mrs. McPherson guilty, so the case against her was dismissed.

More Evidence for Mrs. McPherson

There was still much evidence in support of Mrs. McPherson that had not been heard at the closure and never made the headlines. Those facts are for the most part unknown or overlooked by the public to this very day. When somebody wants to run another story about Aimee, they simply rehash newspaper clippings from years ago, accusations long ago discredited and never proven.

A Strong Voice in Sister's Defense

A person ought to be considered innocent until proven guilty, but Mrs. McPherson received just the opposite treatment. She was treated as guilty until proven innocent.

Raymond L. Cox, researcher and author from Salem, Oregon, spent twenty-five years conducting a thorough investigation into Mrs. McPherson's case. His final conclusions reinforced her innocence. He recorded his findings in a 247-page book entitled *The Verdict Is In*. This book you are reading draws heavily on the authenticity of the Cox book.

The following lengthy quote taken from *The Verdict Is In* gives light on the situation as seen then.

> *In January of 1927, after Asa Keyes cried "Uncle" over the case, some of Mrs. McPherson's friends crowed exuberantly. The evangelist was pleased she would now be able to devote full-time to evangelistic efforts without the interruptions of daily court appearances. Her mother, however, would have preferred to be acquitted by a jury. Minnie Kennedy didn't agree altogether with the assessment of Judge Jacob F. Denny, formerly of the Fifty-eighth Judicial Circuit of Indiana and in 1927 a member of the bar in California.*
>
> *Denny declared:* **The vindication of Mrs. McPherson and Mrs. Kennedy could not be more complete** *(emphasis ours). It is infinitely stronger than if it had been determined by a jury after hearing all the evidence and resulting in an absolute acquittal.*
>
> *A jury passing on the case would naturally be supposed to be unbiased and give an unprejudiced decision. But in the present case, the State of California, with all its machinery, power and prestige, spent many thousands of dollars in the investigation of the charges which*

it had made against these women. The charges, they admitted, were all false. In addition to the ordinary investigation which is made by state officials, this case, by reason of its having excited national interest, was given special attention. For more than half a year, the entire resource of the State of California was devoted to the unearthing of evidence against them. Special agents were employed in great numbers to trace down every remote rumor that might throw light on the case.

All of the evidence collected was reviewed by the officers themselves most interested in procuring a conviction and naturally supposed to be highly hostile to the defendants. This tribunal themselves determined that there was not sufficient evidence against the defendants even to justify placing them on trial before an unprejudiced jury.

Seldom, if ever, in the history of American or English jurisprudence has so signal a vindication been achieved without a single gun being fired by the defendants in their own defense.[22]

It would seem that if the two women had been tried either way, by judge or jury, they would have been highly exonerated. It also seems a matter of honest, though divided, opinion as to which method should have been followed.

How the Case Developed

The District Attorney of Los Angeles showed little interest in pursuing any kidnappers, since he seemed to assume there were none. At the time this preliminary hearing began, the DA was still smarting from the rebuke of California Governor Richardson for convicting innocent people. Raymond L. Cox suggested that Keyes was out to make a name for himself as an invincible prosecutor.

What Was the Specific Charge?

The charge was against both Aimee Semple McPherson and her mother Minnie Kennedy for criminal conspiracy. It was alleged that Mrs. McPherson surreptitiously disappeared, meaning, secretly and purposely. It begs common sense to even think of such a thing. Why would a successful, well-known person of good repute suddenly come up with such a far-out scheme and forsake her family, church and thousands of loyal supporters?

A Lengthy Hearing

This preliminary hearing began on September 27, 1926, and became the longest case of its kind in the history of Los Angeles courts up to that time, with forty-two volumes of manuscript consisting of about 3,500 pages.

Why Keyes?

It was unusual that Keyes, the DA of such a large constituency, would personally conduct the court case while his deputy, Joseph Ryan, sat on the sidelines. Apparently Keyes coveted the publicity and credit for prosecuting in such a highly publicized case.

No Case

In spite of all the so-called arguments, they all fell flat one by one and the case came to an abrupt end on January 10, 1927. After almost ninety consecutive days of testimony, the district attorney admitted that he did not have a case. Yet, Keyes was so vindictive he declared, "*I know she is guilty, but I can't prove it.*"

After the case closed and the newspapers had run all the scoops they could on it, they went on to other "news" with little interest in clearing Aimee's name. Later, Keyes himself was convicted of accepting bribes involving oil scandals and sentenced to serve time in San Quentin Penitentiary.

Lingering Inferences

The mention of Aimee Semple McPherson's name, even to this day, brings up inferences to charges that were false. Unfounded accusations continue to be promoted unknowingly by those who fail to do careful research. Some newspaper articles, movies and talk shows have succeeded in casting a cloud over her reputation that is difficult to erase.

Questions and Answers

The following posed questions and answers help to clarify the issues.

Q. How could such a well-known person disappear from a public beach without being noticed?

A. Mrs. McPherson was in her swimsuit, not the easily recognized Temple uniform. As she was led to the automobile, a long dark coat was slipped over her shoulders.

Q. Did any witnesses see Mrs. McPherson leave the beach?

A. After Aimee's reappearance at least two unrelated people came forward and said that they saw her. On July 8, Harry C. Swift told the press that his observation confirmed Mrs. McPherson's account. It is not known why he did not come forth at the time.

Another man, Edward Waite, a resident of the Sawtelle Soldier's Home, explained on October 21 that on the day of the kidnapping he had taken the street car to Ocean Park, arriving about 2 p.m. and remaining there for about three hours. As he hobbled across the sand with his cane he saw Mrs. McPherson emerging from the surf. He looked again and saw her with a man walking towards an automobile. He was about fifty feet away and saw the man close enough to recognize him again. (He fit the description that Aimee gave of Steve.) Waite then turned and looked towards the tent umbrella, searching in vain for Miss Schaeffer. When he looked back towards the car, it was gone. He attached nothing sinister to what he had seen.

When he heard later about Mrs. McPherson drowning he thought that she must have gone back into the water and drowned after he had seen her by the car. Then, on October 21, the papers reported that a lame man with a cane had been seen on the beach on May 18 with the suggestion that it may have been Ormiston, the former engineer at Angelus Temple radio, who had been accused of running off with Aimee. Waite said, "I decided that it was time for my story to be known, for I was the only lame man on the beach at the time."[23]

Q. Was a ransom demand ever received from kidnappers?

A. Yes. A ransom letter arrived at Angelus Temple. It had been mailed in San Francisco on May 25 and demanded that $500,000 be paid in cash, at once, for the return of Mrs. McPherson. A Temple representative wearing a Temple badge was to bring the money in a paper bag and take a seat in the lobby of the Palace Hotel in San Francisco on Saturday, May 29th, at 11 o'clock. The representative would then be approached and told what to do. The note was signed "Revengers." This was the exact amount that the kidnappers had told Aimee they were demanding. Minnie, still thinking that Aimee had drowned, was inclined not to believe it was genuine. Nevertheless, she turned it over to

Los Angeles Police Detective Herman Cline. The San Francisco police planted two men wearing Temple badges, but no one made contact. Perhaps they suspected the police had been informed. Later, when they looked for the ransom note in the police confidential files, it had "disappeared."[24]

Q. If Mrs. McPherson was wearing a bathing costume when she was kidnapped, how is it she showed up in the desert fully dressed?

A. Would anyone expect her to remain in a bathing suit for a month? Rose, one of her abductors, provided her with clothing and shoes.

Q. How could Aimee possibly cut herself free from her bonds without cutting herself on the can?

A. Aimee demonstrated four times how she turned her back to an open can and rubbed her bonds against the jagged edge to set herself free without cutting herself.

Q. How could Sister walk all that distance in the desert and arrive without showing signs of wear to her clothing?

A. Hosts of desert people backed Sister's story by displaying their own clothing and shoes. Sand is fine and does not cut leather.

Q. How could Sister travel through the desert for that length of time and not show signs of fatigue in her body?

A. Witnesses at Douglas, as well as the Gonzales in Agua Prieta, testified that she was in a state of collapse when she arrived. Other witnesses claimed she looked in bad shape. Her wrists had welts from the bonds and her feet were blistered. Ryan and Cline sought to discredit her, but they did not arrive until Thursday, by which time she was beginning to regain her strength.

Q. Could she really travel all that distance?

A. Desert trackers said that Cline and Ryan toured the desert by car on Friday without seeing her footprints, but others found her tracks up to eighteen miles from Agua Prieta.

Q. Why didn't they find the shack?

A. Contrary to what some have said, several shacks were found in that area. One of them could have been where they held Aimee. Those were prohibition days with a great deal of secret border crossings and bootlegging. Shacks hidden in the sand dunes and sagebrush could be expected. If helicopters had been available it would have been much easier to spot little shacks in the hollows.

Q. How could they take Aimee across the American-Mexican border without being detected?

A. There were rumors of her being seen. The following sighting could have been of Aimee. It came from Sheriff Homer H. Tate of Graham County, Arizona. He did not write to report it until December 24, 1926, when he offered to investigate further for the expected Superior Court trial, which did not materialize. Here is what the sheriff said in his letter as quoted in *The Verdict Is In*, by Raymond Cox:

> *Some days before your appearance in Douglas, Arizona, I happened to be in Bonita, Arizona, on official business, when an automobile bearing California license drove up and inquired the road to Douglas. There was a man driving, and a woman in the back seat was holding on her lap another woman who seemed to be sick. The sick woman was lying on a pillow on the other woman's lap. There is also another man here that saw them and talked to them.*[25]

Sheriff Tate gave the location of Bonita as a little county post office located on the highway in Southern Graham County. The case never got to Superior Court. His letter was buried in the files and never seemed to receive any publicity.

Q. What about the story that Aimee ran away with Kenneth Ormiston, the former radio operator at the temple?

A. When Ormiston heard the rumor he came to Los Angeles, saying that he would cooperate fully to explain his movements and clear Sister of any implications. He satisfied authorities that he could offer no help concerning her whereabouts at that time. But Keyes and the tabloid papers tried to implicate her as the woman who had shacked up with Ormiston at Carmel-on-the-Sea.

Their chief witness turned out to be a proverbial liar whose stories changed by the day. What unearthly reason would a person of Aimee Semple McPherson's caliber and repute have for such a clandestine act? *"Does a spring send forth fresh water and bitter from the same opening?"* (James 3:11). Nothing in all of Mrs. McPherson's previous actions suggested promiscuity.

Mrs. McPherson stands vindicated except in the eyes of those who refuse to admit the facts.

23. The Work Goes On

Some media outlets stated that the kidnapping episode caused Mrs. McPherson's following to drop. Actually, it was the very opposite. At the conclusion of Mrs. McPherson's story of the kidnapping in *The Bridal Call* of August 1926 she adds this footnote:

> *If the Enemy thought to kill the work of God by this persecution, he has certainly overshot his mark. The world, over a path already well beaten, from the four corners of the globe to the doors of Angelus Temple, is hurrying to Los Angeles to see what it is all about. The altars are filled at every service, the baptistery is filled and each week sees scores of people taking a definite stand for the cause of right and uniting with the church to stand shoulder to shoulder with us in the conflict. Our business is preaching the Gospel and in the midst of it all we are calmly and steadfastly continuing with the work of calling men and women to repentance.*

A well-known publication stated that after the kidnapping "her following has dwindled." On the contrary, Mrs. McPherson herself told reporters at the great Boston revival in October 1931 that after her ordeal her church had trebled.[26]

Vindication Tour

Aimee, anxious to thank and assure her followers beyond Los Angeles, took a national tour for three months, speaking twice a day in a different city every three days. She said,

My anxiety was not now so much for the Temple but for the people across the Rockies—those wonderful people who had made the building of Angelus Temple possible. I felt I must go to them and see them face to face and thank them personally for their unwavering loyalty, their abiding faith, their lovely letters and telegrams of encouragement with which they had showered me.[27]

24. Difficult Times

The Great Depression

The great financial crash of 1929 sent shock waves all the way through the 1930s to the beginning of World War II. It affected the whole general populace in cities, towns and countryside. Those dwelling in the great expanse of prairie across America and Canada referred to it as the dirty thirties. The reason for that being because there was no rain. Time after time, farmers looked for rain. They saw clouds on the horizon only to find that they were clouds of dust and tumbleweed. Sometimes they were clouds of grasshoppers that ate everything green and then moved on to devour yet more. Other times it was hail that pounded the life out of their crops.

Feeding the Hungry

When there were no jobs there was no money for food. Angelus Temple still dispensed food and other items for the needy. Such was the volume of need that the financial resources of the Temple were taxed to a crisis point, near bankruptcy. Creditors were threatening to take over the Temple.

Other Problems

When Aimee addressed the Executive Council of the Foursquare Gospel Convention on January 9, 1930, she placed herself before them as a peaceable child of the Lord inviting constructive criticism and advice. She was giving her all, trying her best for the Lord. Even then there were complaints.

There were some interests who looked upon the whole Temple operation as a financial prize to be seized. It is hard to imagine how those with such a view could see themselves operating a church simply for profit.

During the first half of 1930 Aimee continued burning the candle at both ends, preaching and administrating. She was ignoring the advice and pleas of associates and friends to slow down. The nerve specialist called in to examine her told the church council on September 7 that he found Mrs. McPherson attempting ten times more work than anybody should do. She was suffering from a condition where the mind is active and the body is not.

They thought she was dying and so did she, but she rallied and made a remarkable recovery. Within twenty-four hours she had made a miraculous comeback, but by year's end her condition had deteriorated again. When one is restored to health, the same habits that brought on the illness in the first place ought not be repeated.

Aimee said,

The accumulated years of service seemed suddenly to press heavily upon my shoulders with a weight of weariness impossible to bear. I felt crushed to earth with the actual physical pressure of tired nerves and over-taxed muscles. I wondered if there could be an eternity long enough in which to rest. Rest! Rest! Blessed Rest! Rest that brings peace and complete restoration.[28]

Her activities left her broken in health and exhausted. When (daughter) Roberta married William Smythe and (son) Rolph married Lorna Dee Smith, Aimee felt so alone and in need of close companionship. In the midst of all the problems, even family ties with Minnie were overtaxed.

Slow Down—Danger Ahead!

Aimee had completed the music for her production of *The Iron Furnace* and was looking for someone to take the leading role of Pharaoh. Homer Rodeheaver, Billy Sunday's music director, suggested baritone David Hutton. He seemed to have talents that fitted the role, so she hired him.

A Sad Mistake—An Unfortunate Marriage

Aimee in her loneliness considered marrying Hutton. She was forty and he was twenty-nine. His stage career in the 1920s had blended his religious interests with vaudeville. He sang and performed in theaters, as well as giving religious concerts and conducting musical programs in churches. In marrying Aimee, he apparently intended to gain visibility. Reporters challenged her to move ahead with her plans to marry him. It would make a good story for them. Plans were made. One reporter paid airfare for the plane that would take the wedding party to Arizona.

After midnight on the night of September 12, 1931, Aimee and Hutton, with Rolph, Lorna Dee and Harriet Jordan, left for Yuma, Arizona. Shortly after dawn, Harriet Jordan, Aimee's associate and deaconess, performed the wedding ceremony. The Huttons flew back to Los Angeles so that Aimee could preach at the 11 a.m. service. Hutton sang in the choir, but there was no public announcement of their marriage. When the marriage became known, it came as a shock; not all approved, but most held their peace at the time.

A Difficult Story to Tell

This is the most difficult segment of all the story, difficult because it was an impulsive act that turned out to be wrong. Aimee later admitted publicly that she had made a mistake in marrying Hutton. She, who had tried all along to do what was right, had failed.

Those who should have given wise counsel felt sorry for her in her loneliness and acquiesced. As for David Hutton, he seemed to see it as a calculated gamble to enhance his career as well as bring him financial benefits. Trouble was not long in coming. On the wedding night, a reporter happened to mention that a woman named Hazel St. Pierre was threatening to sue Hutton for breach of promise. Poor Aimee; instead of enhancing her situation, she had compounded it. Two days later, St. Pierre filed suit for $200,000 and two other women let it be known that they were also considering suing as well.

Through all Aimee's kidnapping and trial, her followers remained true. This time it was different. Friends and Temple members who loved Aimee found it hard to condone her actions, some because of religious convictions, others because they simply did not approve.

During 1933, Sister Aimee visited Minneapolis, Minnesota, where she conducted meetings at the Municipal Auditorium. The banner over the stage proclaimed: *We Would See Jesus.*

Trying to Make the Best of It

Aimee tried to give Hutton a part in the services, but it wasn't long until he started to press for personal benefits. His long-term aim seemed to be getting Aimee to sign things over to his name.

Matters soon became more incompatible and controversial. Aimee found out that Hutton was making snide remarks about her and the Temple in his role on stage. When she came back from a trip she discovered that he had moved out. They were divorced in 1934 with probably not a tear shed.

Financial Disaster Pending

The financial situation at the Temple was becoming more critical all the time, not only because of the drain at the commissary, but lack of a properly planned budget and general mismanagement.

Minnie, Roberta, and Harriet Jordan had tried unsuccessfully to reign in the situation. Sister's son Rolf was supportive and consistent, but he was too young to assume an important leadership role at that time. The Temple was on the verge of financial collapse if immediate actions were not taken.

Giles Knight

Just in time, Giles Knight, a young Foursquare minister with business background, was appointed business manager. He acted quickly and firmly to staunch the outflow of funds and implemented wise and corrective measures. Aimee's own actions were restricted, and even family members felt alienated. Knight put the entire operation on a cash basis and in 1938 the debt was cleared.

Closing Years of Ministry

Aimee still ministered as she found strength to do so. Many tourists attended along with a strong following of Temple members. In addition, the Foursquare body of churches continued to grow.

Giles Knight's measures had the desired results but had become rather oppressive once the books were balanced and policies put in order. By 1944, his work was done and he resigned early in the year. He had served Aimee and the church well and moved on to head another mission organization. Rolf was now ready to assume greater responsibility, so things were falling into place.

Aimee's Last Service

During the summer of 1944 Aimee was not well, but by the fall she felt well enough to accept an invitation to attend the dedication of a new church in Oakland. She preached her last sermon the evening of Tuesday, September 26, to a capacity crowd of 10,000 in the Oakland Auditorium. The next morning, on September 27, Rolf called for his mother at ten o'clock and found her unconscious in her room. He immediately called for medical assistance, but it was too late. Shortly before noon she was "Promoted to Glory." She was twelve days short of her fifty-fourth birthday.

She had been plagued with insomnia, often having trouble falling asleep after an evening service. They found several capsules on her pillow and on the floor beside her bed. She had kidney trouble also. The coroner stated that the sleeping pills would not have had disastrous effect if it had not been for her kidney ailment.

A quiet moment. Aimee Semple McPherson with son Rolph.

Her son, Dr. Rolf McPherson, said,

I am convinced it was God's time to take her. She had served several lifetimes wrapped up in one, and had undergone great strain from her illness and overwork. I feel sure God said, "It is enough; come on up higher."

25. The Legacy She Left

What Is a Legacy?

A legacy is something one leaves behind when passing from this earthly life. It could be material goods or something of even greater value that will live on to bless generations to come.

Aimee may not have left a great deal of money behind, just over $10,000, but she certainly left a legacy that money could not buy. She was a successful evangelist whose ministry in love and compassion reached out to multitudes of people and brought them to Jesus. He took their broken lives and transformed them, giving them joy and peace on earth and the promise of eternal life in heaven. Just one touch from the Master's hand.

The Touch of the Master's Hand

'Twas battered and scarred, and the auctioneer
Thought it scarcely worth his while
To waste much time on the old violin
But he held it up with a smile.
"What am I bidden, good folk?" he cried,
"Who'll start the bidding for me?
"A dollar—a dollar—then two, only two—
"Two dollars, and who'll make it three?
"Going for three"—but no—
From the room far back, a gray-haired man
Came forward and picked up the bow,
Then wiping the dust from the old violin,

And tightening the loosened strings,
He played a melody pure and sweet
As a caroling angel sings.

The music ceased, and the auctioneer,
With a voice that was quiet and low,
Said, "Now what am I bid for the old violin?"
And he held it up with the bow.
"A thousand dollars—and who'll make it two?
"Two thousand and who'll make it three?
"Three thousand once—three thousand twice—
"And going—and gone," cried he.
The people cheered, but some of them cried.
"We do not understand.
"What changed its worth?"—Quick came the reply,
"The touch of the Master's hand."

And many a man with life out of tune,
And battered and scarred with sin,
Is auctioned cheap, to a thoughtless crowd,
Much like the old violin.
A "mess of pottage"—a glass of wine,
A game—and he travels on:
He is going once—and going twice—
He's going—and almost gone!
But the Master comes, and the foolish crowd
Never quite understand
The worth of a soul, and the change that's wrought
By The Touch of the Master's Hand.

—Myra Brooks Welch, 1921

The following assessment of Aimee and her ministry had
been made at the time of her Lethbridge, Alberta meetings.
It is worth repeating:

Dr. Edith Blumhofer has left us a glowing appraisal of Mrs. McPherson's impact on North America. By mid-year 1920, Sister was becoming a sensation, tapping into deep cultural yearnings, displaying unusual sensitivity to the popular mood.

In June of 1920, the Lethbridge, Alberta, Daily Herald told its readers that the results of Sister's meetings had been "so tremendous that anything like a comprehensive record is impossible to ascertain." It was the same in Dayton, Ohio; Alton, Illinois; and Piedmount, West Virginia—everywhere the response far exceeded expectations.

Could Anything More Be Added?

Scarcely, yet it needs to be noted that this evaluation statement could be repeated over and over again. How many places had Aimee ministered in and therefore how many multiplied thousands of lives had been impacted for good, for time and eternity?

In addition to the individual souls Aimee reached in her meetings, she founded a church organization that continues to carry on her work around the world. It should also be noted that from the time Angelus Temple Commissary opened until Aimee's death it had fed and clothed more than one-and-one-half million people.[29]

The International Church of the Foursquare Gospel

Here are the official statistics:

Foursquare U.S. (2004 Reported)

Number of churches   1,880

| Number of ministers | 6,716 |
| Number of members and adherents | 261,727 |

Foursquare Non-U.S. (2004 Reported)

Number of churches	35,938
Number of ministers	45,477
Number of members and adherents	3,817,105
Non-U.S. countries with Foursquare works	142

What Was Her Secret?

Everybody wants to know the secret of a highly successful person. A short answer is hardly sufficient. It was not just her great talent, as great as that was. It was more than her native ability. The answer is that there was a special anointing from God upon her. Gifts of the Holy Spirit were mightily manifested in her ministry.

Was There Something of Aimee's Own Doing Involved?

Yes and no. The giftings came from God, and yet her own motives and attitude had a great deal to do with it. She always gave glory to God. God's glory cannot be taken to one's self. There is no record of her ever boasting, whatsoever.

Aimee came into her meetings with two essential ingredients: Faith and Fervor. She believed that she was in the will of God and that He would show up, and He did, every time. She counted on that, so much so that she was ready to go out on a limb right in front of everybody. Could we, would we, do the same?

This is bringing us to a final point. Do you want to be used of God? For many of us, if we are honest, the quick answer would be: "Yes." Then why are not more of us gifted and used? The world is in crying need of such people. Perhaps we cannot be trusted to give God the glory and live above reproach.

The Will of God

Are we willing to put ourselves, unconditionally, in God's hands—in His will? Here is a challenge to those who read these words:

> *Seek to know and do the will of God.*
> *There can be no purer motive nor greater*
> *good that you could do.*

Aimee Semple McPherson died on September 27, 1944. She had a dynamic personality and some folk said that when she died her work would come apart at the seams. It did not, but rather grew. Donald Gee, known around the world as a great teacher in the Pentecostal movement, had been a bit wary of her style. But this is what he said five years after her death:

> *Many prophesied, and who can blame them, that the work had been founded upon her personality, but if we accept our Lord's test that "by their fruits ye shall know them," the results are all in her favor, for the work has only deepened and increased in every way since her death, and the undeniably good fruit is there* (Cox, p. 238).

Resting place of Aimee Semple McPherson. Forest Lawn
Memorial Park, Glendale, California.

Appendix

The Unknown God

Several years ago, my wife and I were privileged to be part of a tour group on a trip to Europe and the Middle East. There was a stopover in Athens, Greece, for a couple of days, with time for sightseeing. From our hotel room in downtown Athens we could look up the nearby hillside and see the Acropolis with the remains of the Parthenon and other ancient ruins.

One afternoon our tour bus stopped at the foot of the hill and a guide led us up the windswept slope, explaining details of the relics. About halfway to the summit she motioned to a rocky knoll over to one side called Mars Hill. It was there that the court of Areopagus used to meet and discuss religious matters. We decided to go back and see it for ourselves the next day.

At the base of Mars Hill a large metal plaque was secured to the face of the rock. The plaque bore an inscription from the 17th chapter of the Acts of the Apostles. It was the text of the speech given before the members of the Areopagus court by the Apostle Paul on his first visit to Athens. We climbed up the rocky slope and stood on the dome of rock where the court used to meet centuries before.

Athenian Culture, Religion

Athens was the focal point of art, architecture, literature and politics during Greece's golden age. Paul and his party of helpers had crossed into Europe from Asia Minor to introduce Christianity to the people of Europe.

After planting churches in Philippi, Thessalonica and Berea, Paul continued south to Athens. While waiting there for Silas and Timothy to join him he observed the Athenian culture and religion. His heart was stirred as he saw how the city was given over to idolatry. They had raised up idols to a multitude of gods and, just to be sure they did not miss one, they erected an altar to "The Unknown God."

Paul's first contact in a new city was usually the Jewish synagogue because they worshipped Almighty God, the creator. It was his point of contact with the Jews. But there was no such common religious ground with idolaters.

What followed is a classic example of communicating the gospel to a people who had no Bible background. Paul, an able debater, skillfully met them on their own ground and introduced them to the true God. Standing in their midst he said,

> *"Men of Athens, I observe that you are very religious in all respects. For while I was passing through and examining the objects of your worship, I also found an altar with this inscription, 'TO AN UNKNOWN GOD.' Therefore what you worship in ignorance, this I proclaim to you. The God who made the world and all things in it, since He is Lord of heaven and earth, does not dwell in temples made with hands; nor is He served by human hands, as though He needed anything, since He Himself gives to all people life and breath and all things; and He made from one man every nation of mankind to live on all the face of the earth, having determined their appointed times and the boundaries of their habitation, that they would seek God, if perhaps they might grope for Him and find Him, though He is not far from each one of us; for in Him we live and*

move and exist, as even some of your own poets have said, 'For we also are His children.' Being then the children of God, we ought not to think that the Divine Nature is like gold or silver or stone, an image formed by the art and thought of man. Therefore having overlooked the times of ignorance, God is now declaring to men that all people everywhere should repent, because He has fixed a day in which He will judge the world in righteousness through a Man whom He has appointed, having furnished proof to all men by raising Him from the dead" (Acts 17:22-31 NASB).

At that point, the idolaters rejected his message, but some joined Paul and believed. Among them was Dionysius, the Areopagite, a woman named Damarius, and others with them. When the Athenians were made aware of the identity and claims of the "Unknown God," they were compelled to make a decision. Would they accept Him or would they reject Him? That same question faces all of us. God has revealed Himself through general revelation, that is, the existence of our world and universe. Not only that, but He has given us special revelation in His Word, the Bible, by His Son, Jesus Christ, and by the preaching of the gospel.

He invites us to test Him, to try Him. *"Oh, taste and see that the LORD is good"* (Psalm 34:8). Will you, dear reader, consider accepting Him as your Lord and Savior? Simply ask Him to forgive your sins and invite Him into your life.

For the wages of sin is death, but the gift of God is eternal life in Christ Jesus our Lord (Romans 6:23).

Follow up your decision by an honest attempt to live a Christian life. Associate yourself with other believers and be consistent in your daily Bible reading and prayer.

Endnotes

[1] Foursquare Online, p. 3 of 3. March 8, 2005, on-line posting, http://www.foursquare.org/landing_pages/8,3.html.

[2] A. C. Valdez Sr., *Fire on Azusa Street* (Costa Mesa, California: Gift Publications, 1980) 75,76.

[3] Aimee Semple McPherson, *The Personal Testimony of Aimee Semple McPherson* (Los Angeles, California: Heritage Dept. of the Foursquare Church, 1998) 31,32.

[4] McPherson, *The Personal Testimony of Aimee Semple McPherson*, 34.

[5] Aimee Semple McPherson, *This Is That* (Los Angeles, California: Bridal Call Publishing House: 1919) pp. 113-115.

Ian Easterbrook, *Wellington County History*, Vol. 9 (Fergus, Ontario: Wellington County Historical Society, 1996) 22,23.

[6] Easterbrook, 46-47.

[7] Edith Blumhofer, *Aimee Semple McPherson: Everybody's Sister* (Grand Rapids, Michigan: Wm. B. Eerdmans Publishing Co., 1993) 142.

[8] Blumhofer, 151,152.

[9] Blumhofer, 153.

[10] Douglas Rudd, *When the Spirit Came Upon Them* (Mississauga, Ontario: The Pentecostal Assemblies of Canada, 2002) 295-299.

[11] McPherson, *The Personal Testimony of Aimee Semple McPherson*, 48,50.

[12] Blumhofer, 190.

[13] McPherson, *The Personal Testimony of Aimee Semple McPherson*, 56,57.

[14] Blumhofer, 169.

[15] Charles S. Price, *And Signs Followed* (Plainfield, New Jersey: Logos International, 1972) 35.

[16] Price, 36-44.

[17] Blumhofer, 199.

[18] McPherson, *The Personal Testimony of Aimee Semple McPherson*, 58.

[19] Blumhofer, 235,236.

[20] McPherson, *The Personal Testimony of Aimee Semple McPherson*, 60.

[21] Blumhofer, 287.

[22] Raymond L. Cox, *The Verdict Is In* (Los Angeles, California: Research Publishers, 1983) 10,11.

[23] Cox, 18,19.

[24] Cox, 41,42.

[25] Cox, 34.

[26] Cox, 237.

[27] McPherson, *The Personal Testimony of Aimee Semple McPherson*, 67,68.

[28] McPherson, *The Personal Testimony of Aimee Semple McPherson*, 74.

[29] Cox, 241.